How We Co

MSc papers in Psycho-Social Dynamics and Affective Neuroscience

David Charles Rowan

Contents:

Title: Page

Acknowledgements 5

Foreword 7

Introduction 9

Is There A Basis In Neuroscience For NLP ? 13

Forming an Attachment to Attachment Theory:
A Journey To An Emergent Understanding. 41

A Place To Belong: Investigating The Relationship
Between Landscape And Identity. 69

What Roles May Discourse, Narrative And Literalism
Play In The Making And Resolution Of Conflict ? 105

Determinism And Agency In Affective Neuroscience:
A Psycho-Social Perspective. 127

Post Script 195

Acknowledgements

For Nigel Williams; my inspiring and infinitely patient guide and tutor ...

Thank You !

A huge thank you to the courageous participants of these studies; your willingness to explore your relationship with your history in the present will undoubtedly help others in their future.

Thank You !

For the progressive and somewhat experimental Psycho-Social Studies unit at the University of the West of England; Nigel Williams, Simon Clarke, Paul Hoggert and Lita Crociani-Windland ...

Thank You !

Foreword

by
Dr. Ania Lian
Charles Darwin University, Darwin, NT, Australia

For those engaged in an on-going search for "outside the box" tools in order to better understand our human condition, this book, *Determinism and agency in affective neuroscience,* offers an opportunity to engage, with the author, in a journey which explores cutting-edge discoveries in brain science in relation to age-old questions such as free will, agency and the nature of reality itself.

The book appears at a time when cross-disciplinary thinking challenges the routines of traditional research schools, pushing studies in a direction where the representatives of seemingly incommensurable fields of sciences, such as physics and biology, or, indeed, neuroscience and spirituality, frequently meet on the same symposium panels discussing and building on epistemological differences and commonalities. At the same time, progressively, mindfulness practices are being introduced to schools and workplaces throughout the Western world, with policy-makers and business executives drawing on a new body of evidence demonstrating a link between one's overall compassionate disposition and productivity.

The current concepts of well-being as a state, where individuals are given opportunities to self-actualise, relate to others while also exercising a fair degree of autonomy and control, are seen to contradict longstanding truths where these higher order emotional states were seen as secondary to more basic human needs such as the need for water, air or food. Today we know that the brain registers rejection the same way as it registers physical pain. Our thoughts and emotions are two aspects of the same process: how we feel affects the signals the brain sends to the body in order to generate an appropriate protective response. In short, how we feel influences how we think, which then impacts on our physiology and our general disposition.

The understanding that "we feel therefore we are" (Damasio & Immordino-Yang, 2009) may well summarise the extent to which our will plays a role in our fate and daily experiences. It is not uncommon that research today provides evidence for understandings which previously were seen as mere conjectures or just the product of fantasy. It is the combined imagination of scientists, philosophers and creative authors that pushes the boundaries of the universe as we know it and, in so doing, provides science with new questions. I believe that it is the purpose of the current book to engage the reader in a journey of discovery through research and questions which provoke reflection, inspire imagination and challenge the terms in which we frame the concepts of self and other.

Introduction

The collection of papers within this book are the complete body of work from my MSc in Psycho-Social Studies, undertaken at the University of the West of England (UWE), Bristol, between 2008 and 2010.

The dissertation thesis, Determinism and Agency in Affective Neuroscience; a Psycho-Social Perspective, is, in my opinion, the principle of my writing ability to date. It not only explores the neuroscience of fate and free-will, it also addresses the dilemma of nature verses nurture and resolves this with a quadrvium; a non-linear dynamical system comprising epigenetic and ontogentic potentials, cultural and socio-affective neuro-conditioning, an autobiographical past and an anticipated future trajectory, which form a synthesis of self in the present moment.

The papers from the preliminary modules of the degree paved the way for the dissertation research; setting the scene and introducing concepts which are then further explored. Although the topics of the modules were seemingly distinct and different on the surface, a unifying theme emerged as I progressed through the MSc which I found personally illuminating. It would be no exaggeration to say that what I discovered during this study has determined the orientation of my research ever since and interpersonal neurobiology has become the focus of my client practice and personal interest.

The 4 modules and their papers are:

Affect, Emotion and Society:
'Is there a basis in Neuroscience for NLP ?'

Psychoanalytic Psychotherapy:
'Forming an Attachment to Attachment Theory: a journey to an emergent understanding.'

Researching Beneath the Surface:
'A Place to belong: investigating the relationship between landscape and identity.'

Conflict, Communication and Transformation:
'What roles may discourse, narrative and literalism play in the making and resolution of conflict ?'

Dissertation thesis:
'Determinism and Agency in Affective Neuroscience: a Psycho-Social perspective'

'Is there a basis in Neuroscience for NLP ?' ... explores how neuroscience theory underpins and supports NLP practice and gives an overview on areas where these two approaches find common ground. It also highlights where NLP concepts and neuroscience findings differ. In addition, for a reader new to these topics, this paper also serves as an introduction to brain anatomy and affective neuroscience.

'Forming an Attachment to Attachment Theory: a journey to an emergent understanding.' ... follows the pathway from an encounter with Attachment theory as a complete novice to being an impassioned advocate for this model and therapeutic approach in psychotherapy. The paper concludes with four short case studies, presenting a surface perspective of attachment theory and a beneath the surface investigation.

'A Place to belong: investigating the relationship between landscape and identity.' ... in a journey of twists and turns, this paper begins life as a research paper investigating the dynamics of a conflict between two community groups; Pagans and Christians, in Avebury Henge, Wiltshire. Following Psycho-Social qualitive research methods, a different, unconscious agenda emerged ...

One of the qualitive research methods, 'photo matrix', involved showing a small group of fellow students photographs of Avebury from both the 'Christian' and 'Pagan' perspectives. The research value comes from noting their emotional and affective responses to the photographs. To represent the Christian side of the community I presented photographs of the church, the school, giving the impression of an ordinary quintessential English village without any hint of the ancient stone circle. The Pagan view comprised a series of photographs of the stones without any of the furniture of modernity. While noting the student's reactions to seeing the photographs, Professor Simon Clarke pointed out that, here is a project researching beneath the surface of a community conflict, and yet not one photograph had any people in it; they were all photographs of landscape and environment, but no people. I suddenly realised that, unconsciously, I was not researching community tensions at all, but the relationship between ourselves and the landscape in which we reside. We are used to the idea that we humans shape the world around us, but is the converse also true ? Are we psychologically shaped by out landscape ?

'What roles may discourse, narrative and literalism play in the making and resolution of conflict ?' ... this short, formative paper explores the relationship between experience, language and behaviour.

'Determinism and Agency in Affective Neuroscience: a Psycho-Social perspective' ... the preliminary papers of this MSc form a foundation for this considerable research project. Does the architecture of the brain determine our character, and does our biology or our formative environment determine the architecture of our brain ? What roles do ontogentic factors and real-time experience play in further sculpting and shaping the brain, or indeed, our character and sense of who we are ?

The research yields fresh insights into how we become who we are and presents a 4-part model in response to the dualism of nature versus nurture, in addition to proposing an agentic environment. Whether these findings are considered to be controversial, illuminating, esoteric, or just plain logical, they are each worthy avenues for further investigation.

On a personal level, the MSc in Psycho-Social Studies did not just open new doors of understanding ; it created them, generating perspectives hitherto unhinted at out of thin air and ushering my feet along new pathways of comprehending the dynamics of the human condition. We are not creatures of fate, and neither are we creatures of free-will. We are unfolding narratives of conditioned, and structured polysemy, instinctively searching for ways to re-verse our story. This book turns another page in the story of how we become who we are.

Is there a basis in Neuroscience for NLP ?

Reflections on my practice from
my participation in the AES programme

This is a formative paper, exploring the neuroscientific basis behind the emerging field of NLP. Taking a Psycho-Social approach also requires that the material is viewed not just with regard to the findings of this study, but also, that it is placed within a broader context of personal reflexivity and society.

The paper will describe the journey of my introduction to neuroscience and how the methodology of my private client practice been changed from what I have learned. The primary models of NLP will be outlined and the NLP meaning of the word 'language' defined. Three case study examples from my practice experience will be presented to illustrate specific points and to investigate the possible correlations between neuroscience and NLP. This will include providing an overview of brain anatomy and an example of NLP methodology. In addition, I feel it is important to state that I have no philosophical allegiance to any particular therapeutic approach; neither am I partisan towards the field of NLP, having no interest in affording it any undue favour. In practice, my first and only interest is that of the wellbeing of my client.

Introducing Neuroscience

The first train of thought inspired from the initial AES lectures that introduced neuroscience, was a reflection on my level of knowledge, which was very poor. This struck a chord of discomfort because I have fifteen years experience as a teacher of NLP and yet I found I knew very little of the topic from which NLP has taken the first of its three names; Neuro Linguistic Programming.

All I had absorbed from my own training, and subsequent professional development, was that NLP has its eye focussed on both the cognitive elements of linguistics and transformational grammar, and also upon the unconscious programming dynamics of hypnosis and hypnotherapy. The neuro part of the name was only discussed in terms of the central nervous system and representational systems. Memories were said to be encoded in different sensory systems and stored in the unconscious, but there was not one occasion in which the anatomy of the brain or the biology of how this occurs was discussed. As the first lecture on neuroscience came to an end, I was unable to decide if I was more astounded to find that much of the neuroscience seemed to support the tenets of NLP, or whether my astonishment was born from the emerging realisation that this area may possibly be overlooked by the NLP community.

Survey: Neuroscience in NLP Training

Instinctively, I feel that the relationship between neuroscience and NLP is important, so I decided to conduct an internet micro-survey to see if I could gauge the extent to which NLP gives attention to, or ignores, the root of its name. Ten websites were randomly selected and the following question asked:

> I'm just about to begin to write a paper for an Msc in Psychosocial Studies and I wondered if I might ask, have you ever encountered an NLP training course that taught Neuroscience or the biology of the brain in an explicit way ? If you run, or design, NLP training, do you include Neuroscience or the biology of the brain in an explicit way and what are your reasons for doing so, or not ... ?

I received six replies. Four said they did not cover the topic in an explicit way and had no knowledge of any courses that did. I was referred to an author by one reply and to a research project at Surrey University by another: http://www.nlpresearch.org/

It would appear that while some ground is tentatively covered in NLP training, the teaching of neuroscience that stands at the forefront of the discipline is woefully overlooked. This may be because there is only an interest amongst NLP practitioners and trainers to replicate what they themselves have been taught and to only direct NLP research into the areas of language and hypnotic programming, to the exclusion of neuroscientific theory, which would appear to be counter to the adventurous and exploratory spirit of NLP (Andreas 1989, introducion).

Or, it may be because the Neuro part of the name, Neuro Linguistic Programming, has no place in this field. Is there a basis in neuroscience for NLP ?

The Primary Models of NLP

There are a number of metaphorical frameworks, or models, employed within NLP (Bandler in Andreas 1991, foreword). A core model of NLP is to view thinking in one of two linguistic levels: surface structure and deep structure (Grinder and Bandler 1975, p. 137). The term surface structure is a phrase denoting the words used to express thought, while deep structure refers to the meanings and experiences associated with the words. Often these associations and experiences are unconscious, as is the word-selection process (Bandler and Grinder, 1975 p. 22).

In an NLP consultation, the practitioner will ask the client questions in a certain manner in order to elicit meanings and associations attached to the wording so that deeper issues can be reviewed and new possibilities explored (Bandler and Grinder, 1975 p. 41). NLP practitioners are taught that the deep structure associations are embedded within the unconscious memory in the form of representational systems; modalities of neural information, namely sights, sounds, and feelings (Bandler and Grinder, 1979 p. 82). In NLP these are called visual, auditory and kinaesthetic and some training schools also teach the practitioner to utilise olfactory and gustatory information (Indigo Eagle NLP Training, 2009). Auditory can refer to either external or internally generated sounds, such as the memory of sounds or internal narrative. Kinaesthetic can refer to either emotions, sensations or both (Stone, 2009).

The NLP term for bringing deeper associations to the surface is known as Meta Model Questioning. (Bandler and Grinder, 1979 p. 70). Open questions are phrased to elicit specific neural information. The objective is not merely to discover the client's subjective experience, it is to build a linguistic map of the client's model with a view to making adjustments within its landscape, thereby altering the client's subjective experience of the issue (Bandler and Grinder, 1975 p. 45).

Eliciting the neurological deep structure of a client's experience may typically take the following form (Bandler and Grinder, 1981, p. 61):

'When you think of that experience, what do you see ?'
'What do you feel ?'
'Are there any sounds associated with that experience ?'
'What kinds of things are you saying to yourself as you experience that ?'
'What do you say to yourself as you think of that now ?'
'Become aware of other sensations, how does your body feel ?'
'Notice your breathing speed ... the tension in your hands ... any smells or tastes associated with that experience'.

A second core model of NLP is that of the Milton Model. While observing the language patterns of the American hypnotherapist Milton Erickson, Richard Bandler and John Grinder found that Milton was able to achieve the opposite orientation to that of the Meta Model. He delivered language to a client, at the surface level of expression, in such a manner that it embedded itself into the deep structures of the client's experience. He achieved this by deliberately employing ambiguity in his sentence structures which, when delivered in certain tones of voice, for the client would prompt an inner search for meaning. As the client begins their creative participation, their attention is turned inwards and the state of consciousness is altered (Grinder and Bandler 1975, page 17).

When used together, the Meta and Milton models provide the practitioner with the means to elicit information from the deep structure of a client and bring it to the surface level of expression and/or deliver language at the surface in a manner that will send it directly into the deep structure of the client.

The Meta Model & Milton Model Illustrated

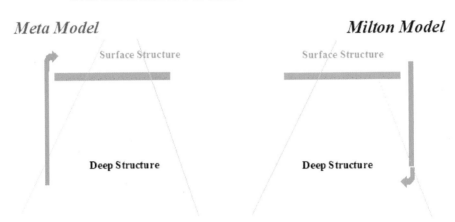

Hypnotic language patterns differ from ordinary speech. How their application may alter states of consciousness and regulate affect is a question that exceeds the scope of this paper and it is my intention to conduct a deeper investigation in a paper to follow.

Language in NLP

In NLP, the term 'language' is used to denote all form of human communication, not only words. NLP practitioners are taught to incorporate specific tones of voice, body postures and how to adjust the speed of their speech in order to induce altered states of consciousness.

38% TONE OF VOICE

TONALITY

QUALITY

PITCH

TEMPO

TONE

VOLUME

SPEED

TIMBRE

PACE

analogue

55%

BODY LANGUAGE

PROPRIOCEPTION

BREATHING

EYE MOVEMENT

SKIN COLOUR

POSTURE

MOVEMENT

MUSCLE TONUS

7% Digital - words

(illustration: Harrison 2001, p.44)

The Territory of the Map: Brain Anatomy, Memory and Unconscious Programming in Neuroscience and NLP

The understanding in NLP is that memories are not recorded on some kind of photo-plate in the brain, but rather, that memories are discretely encoded and stored in different modes of the individual's neurology (Bandler 1985, p. 21). I was pleasantly surprised to learn in the first neuroscience lecture that findings from this field confirm that memory is distributive. The NLP model of memory encoding appears to correlate with the implicit memory structure of the amygdala (Wilkinson 1996, p.25). During my research for this paper I was introduced to another model of brain anatomy that suggests a basis in neuroscience for NLP theory. This additional model that refers to the evolution of its architecture is known as the Triune Brain (Cozolino 2002, p. 8). MacLean's theory suggests there are three distinct regions within the brain's topography which have evolved from the origins of life and remain adaptive, undergoing a constant 'use-dependent development' (Cozolino 2002, p. xv). Each of these regions performs a different type of function, with new layers becoming increasingly complex (Cozolino 2002, p. 8):

The Reptilian Brain is a core region which has changed little through its evolutionary history and is responsible for activation, arousal, reproductive drives and the homeostasis of the organism. One area of NLP developed by Ernest Rossi is that of Psychobiology. Rossi worked with Milton Erickson towards the end of Erickson's life and in 1987 published the Psychobiology of Mind Body Healing (Rossi 1993). This pioneering work proposed models of hypnotic language that would interact directly with the visceral and physiological levels of experience. It may be the case that Psychobiology works with the Reptilian Brain.

Wrapped around the reptilian brain is the Paleomammalian Brain, or Limbic System and its functions are that of learning, memory and emotion. This area of the brain also appears to correlate with the theories of both Rossi; Psychobiology and Milton; programming the unconscious.

The higher and more recent layer is the Neomammalian Brain. This region, the cerebral cortex and the corpus callosum, is the area responsible for conscious thought and self awareness and would seem to correlate with the cognitive features of the NLP Meta Model and transformational grammar (Bandler and Grinder 1975, p. 27).

However, further study reveals that MacLean's model of the Triune Brain is somewhat simplistic. Each region continues to evolve and adapt, and they are interconnected by a complex network of bands of nerve fibres that connect not only the left and right hemispheres horizontally, but also vertically as well. It is estimated that the brain contains around, '...100 billion neurons; each one connected to its neighbours by aproximately 5000 synapses. A million new connections can be made or broken each second.' (Philips 2009, p.29). The brain can organise and prioritise information and regulate the entire body while navigating the external environment successfully, in milliseconds (Damasio 2000, p.67).

The Limbic System is responsible for the emergency response system of the brain. It functions precognitively, inducing an immediate and total brain-body response. During an emergency, the cortex, where a more measured view may be taken, is informed while the amygdala activates the response process. The amygdala is the storehouse for unconscious conditioned emotional patterns and responses. These are often formed in the first three years of life, before the long-term memory and explicit memory systems of the hippocampus develop (Wilkinson 2006, p.25). NLP also teaches that the unconscious stores conditioned responses and calls this process Anchoring (Bandler and Grinder, 1979 p. 79)
The precognitive stimulus, before it is experienced in awareness as an emotion, is known in neuroscience as affect. The manner in which affect is regulated, whether it manifests in different emotional forms such as panic, fear, care, rage (Panksepp 2008, p.124), is cast by the template or 'emotional repertoire' built from having survived traumatic experiences (Wilkinson 2006, p.25). The amygdala is both the seat of reactive responses and learning (Wilson, p.25), and of an evolving and adaptive system. This implies that it is possible to recondition the limbic system to react or respond in different ways (Fonagy et al 2004, p.93). This potential for adaptation correlates exquisitely with the core principles of NLP (James and Woodsmall 1988, p.96).

Once an emotional response has begun, commands are sent to the body and other regions of the brain by two systems; chemical and electrochemical. The resultant change in the system is global and it is possible for the state of the entire organism to be modified from a response triggered by a relatively small area of the brain (Damasio 2000, p.67). Much of the orientation of NLP technique focuses on state control using cognition. Frequently, a client is taught to use what is effectively a tool for affect regulation, via an internal narrative language (Bandler and Grinder 1981, p. 62). In *Affect Regulation and the Origin of the Self*, Schore affirms that there is a correlation between the mechanisms of affect and cognition (Schore 1994, p. 315). Folensbee (2007) cites LeDoux (1996), suggesting that the process of recovering implicit memories, bringing implicit or unconscious memories into conscious awareness, also brings them into the explicit memory system. He writes:

> This process is not the same as uncovering a repressed memory; a conscious memory which was previously driven from awareness by psychodynamic defences which may later be recalled. It is hypothesised that in moments of severe trauma the hippocampus is deactivated and the event itself is not encoded in declarative memory, (Folensbee 2007, p.118).

During such an event, the memory is stored within the amygdala, the region which has come to the fore with regard to regulating and controlling the system's responses. Psychobiology suggests that the memory of an event experienced during an altered state of consciousness is stored in a part of the unconscious which is irretrievable after a return to the normal state. This is referred to by Rossi as State Dependent Memory (Rossi 1993, p.80).

Case Study Example: One

The neuroscience taught on the AES course has opened new perspectives for me, enriching my understanding of my craft, even at this early stage of investigation. One insight emerging from this study is that NLP technique appears to be more effective when dealing with issues that carry an affective charge. I would like to illustrate this possibility by recounting my experience of a corporate client I shall call 'Peter'.

Peter was the HR director of one of the city of London's leading companies and had asked me to assist him in accelerating the speed with which he could further develop his golfing skills. I met up with him and one of his colleagues at a London golf club and spent almost an hour using a selection of techniques which will be discussed further in this paper. At the end of the consultation, as we were preparing to part company, Peter mentioned that he was feeling nervous about another matter. It transpired that he was to give his first after dinner speech that night. The occasion was his best friend's 50th birthday and the importance of the occasion added to the pressure. We had used all but ten minutes of our time allocated for the use of the room, and so I asked if he could spare a moment before testing our morning's work on the green. In a state of heightened awareness and creative spontaneity, I succinctly guided him through a series of brief techniques that ordinarily would take at least a whole afternoon to accomplish. The situation was highly charged from his distress and the accumulated tension was being released though a symphony of emotions ranging from fear and panic to relief and uncontrollable giggles.

It was more than a week before I had the opportunity to talk to Peter and ask how he had found the work we had undertaken and what the results were. He reported that he was a little disappointed with the outcome he found on the golf course and the work we did seemed to have hardly made any difference. The verdict at this stage was not just that it was not worth the time we had spent but also that perhaps the efficacy of NLP may be questioned. Peter said that he was not particularly bothered by this finding because he only saw the golfing skills work as an entertaining experiment which carried almost no emotional investment for him. However, rather than tell me the news with an air of despondency, he could hardly contain a sense of excitement as he began to recount his experience of the after dinner speech. He was astounded to find that it went far better than he would ever have expected. As he finished his speech he won a standing ovation and was asked afterwards if he was a barrister because his manner and delivery were so professional. Within a week he had received two further invitations to speak again.

NLP and Neuroscience Correlations of Case Study Example: One

Peter's response could be explained in a variety of ways from both an NLP and neuroscience perspective:

Rapport building:

Sufficient rapport was not established during the golf skills work and this was reflected in the poor results obtained. One of the tenets of NLP is that in order to facilitate an environment within which change or transformation may occur, the practitioner must have a clear and unpolluted perception of the client's model of reality. Entering the client's model is called 'pacing'. Once pacing has been established, the practitioner then leads the client towards resolution by changing their own internal state (Bandler and Grinder, 1979 p. 79). There is insufficient space within this paper for a deeper exploration of 'pace and lead', however, on the surface it appears very similar to the model of 'transference and counter transference' found in psychoanalytic psychotherapy (Bateman and Holmes 1995, p95). A basis for the concept of utilising rapport via pacing and leading is supported in neuroscience by the discovery of mirror neurons in 1995 by Jeannerod, Arbib, Rizzolatti and Sakata (Cozolino 2002, p.186). Mirror neurons fire when an action is either performed or observed and may also play a role in forms of procedural learning, namely modelling, and synchronous collective actions such as dancing.

State elicitation:

The fact that Peter had only a little emotional investment with the golf-skills project could be attributed to the position that playing golf held within his personal value system. Alternatively, it could be attributed to my inability to draw his emotional relationship with playing golf to the surface for re-direction.

25

Anchoring:

Anchoring is a technique described by Anthony Robbins as Neuro Associative Conditioning (sporthealth4u.com, 2009.), in which the practitioner includes a new added element into the client's experience while the client is recalling a memory or experiencing a particular state (Bandler and Grinder, 1979 p. 83). The added element is a neurological stimulus, most usually kinaesthetic, such as a hand touch on the client's shoulder, but it can also a visual picture or an audio stimulus such as a word or specific tone of voice. The ubiquitous phenomenon of anchors being 'set up' and then 'fired' can be observed in the comedian's catch phase, the lovers' song and the bread shop's allure.

In the light of neuroscience, however, it would seem that the issue of the golf skills did not carry a powerful affective charge for Peter, whereas the after dinner speech did. Affect may be thought of as the precognitive sensation of the intensity of experience (Deleuze 1978, p.1), and there was a high degree of affect involved which manifested for Peter in a set of fears; fear of failure, social embarrassment and letting down his dearest friend. It might be the case that the potential for change and transformation within NLP technique is dependent on the magnitude of affective charge. If one were to rephrase this suggestion using NLP terminology, one would say; it is dependent on the intensity of the state experienced by the client in the moment of the work being done. Richard Bandler, one of the founders of NLP, refers to this as the propulsion system (Callaghan, 2009). One perspective of NLP is that much of the work is focussed upon the orientation of the client's internal direction (James and Woodsmall 1988, p.148). In helping the client to alter the trajectory, the subsequent chain of responses, actions and reactions open new pathways which lead the client to an entirely new destination.

The Illusion of Representation: Challenges from Neuroscience to NLP

It may appear at this stage of the paper that neuroscience does offer a supportive basis for NLP and a judgement may be drawn. However, it remains inconclusive and any such deduction may be premature. Neuroscience also offers challenges to NLP which may require that NLP re-examines its model of subjective experience and that it too may have been caught in the illusion of the Cartesian split (Edelman and Tononi 2000, p.4).

For example, navigating reality requires not only that we move safely through space; we must also manage ourselves in time. It has been shown that we have the capacity for explicit and implicit memory; a relationship with the past, and an adaptable response system that enables us to deal with the present in both an automotive, emotional and highly complex way. Edelman and Tononi assert that although it may be tempting to say that the brain represents information, such as the memories of images and sounds, there is no mechanism within the brain for doing this. Memory is distributive and the core consciousness is not organised by sensory modality, such as visual or auditory. Domasio states, 'Core consciousness can be used by any sensory modality and by the motor system to generate knowledge about any object or movement' (Domasio 2000, p218). Neural signals do not carry a pre-selected code for encoding and '... there is no homunculus in the head to read the message', (Edelman and Tononi 2000, p.94). Moreover, the global mapping system, related to the hippocampus, basal ganglia and cerebellum, is not a store for fixed or coded attributes to be recalled and assembled in a replicative manner, but rather, they are the result of a continual process of synaptic changes that involve rehearsed selection among sets of pathways with similar outputs (Edelman and Tononi, p.97). Edelman and Tononi concur with Pinker that while language lends itself to the symbolism of describing experience in representational terms, the denotations for words are concentrated in the neocortex (Pinker 2007, p.332).

Navigating the Map: Introducing the Neuroscience of How Consciousness Emerges.

The Time Line theory of James and Woodsmall (James and Woodsmall 1988, p15) finds a parallel in Domasio's assertion that human consciousness has a sense of a self that is both permanent and evolving towards an unfolding or developing future (Domasio 2000, p219). In each given moment there are thousands of possible directions, or neural pathways for our thoughts to take. Dennet likens these countless choices to a pandemonium state of consciousness within which a process of selection among many possible options takes place (Dennet 1993, p241). Edelman and Tononi describe Selectionism and Reentry; an ongoing process during which neural pathways are reactivated and reinforced. If reactivation does not occur, or becomes more infrequent, then the route of that pathway can degenerate (Edelman and Tononi 2000, p.85). For those engaged in the practice of talking therapy in a general sense, it is both reassuring and potentially fruitful to have contemporary neuroscience confirm that the application of language can influence changes in neural activity (Cozolino 2002, p.146) and neural pathways can be strengthened by repetition (Folensbee 2007, p.117). This also lends support to the core principles of NLP; that language can be applied to assist a person to bring resolution and transformation to an issue or problem in a manner that does not always necessitate an exploration of the client's history and may be achieved in a faster time frame than other approaches within the talking therapy arena (Bandler and Grinder 1979, p.101).

An Example of NLP Methodology

I would now like to illustrate this using one of the methodologies from NLP practice (Harrison 2001, p.29). The NLP practitioner:

a) Gains rapport with the client.

b) Identifies the problem for which the client is seeking assistance and elicits its linguistic deep structure; the Meta Model.

c) Identifies, together with the client, the ideal solution/resolved state and checks thoroughly that any such change will be beneficial for the client as a whole and that both the conscious and unconscious mind of the client will find such changes acceptable.

d) Guides the client through a process of change and transformation, systematically utilising a series of cognitive and/or hypnotic tools and techniques.

e) Anchors the changes into the client's perception of the future so that the transformation will endure and remain part of the client's adapted reality.

Wilfred Bion is one of many authors from a diverse spectrum of disciplines who have written on the act or art of transformation; to move to a form beyond that held in the present (Bleandonu 1994 p.199). The chaotic epicentre of the formless moment of change, between the deconstruction of the old and the generation of the new, also rests at the heart of NLP (Harrison 2001, p.245). A deceptively simplistic metaphor for illustrating this process can be found in a neuro-disruptive technique from the canon of NLP: the Pattern Interrupt.

The NLP practitioner may utilise the pattern interrupt technique to disrupt a habit or repeating behaviour. For the NLP practitioner, the content of what is repeating is less important than the process; the sequence of the steps of the behaviour that link together to form the repetitive action. As the client demonstrates the repeated action, the practitioner suddenly interrupts the behaviour. This momentarily causes the client to become bewildered and confused. At that precise moment of controlled pandemonium, the practitioner directs the client's thinking with short concise instructions, towards the new goal or behaviour (Harrison 2001, p.20).

A Simple Illustration of The Pattern Interrupt Technique

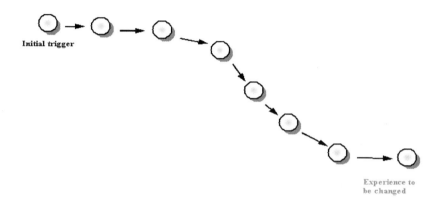

Usual pattern

Initial trigger

Experience to be changed

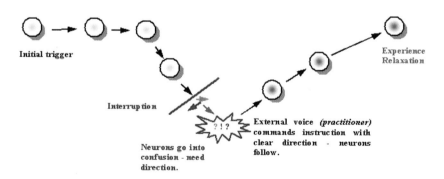

Pattern Interrupt

Initial trigger

Interruption

?!?

Neurons go into confusion - need direction.

External voice *(practitioner)* commands instruction with clear direction - neurons follow.

Experience Relaxation

One pattern interrupt method is a hypnotic arm-leverage technique, sometimes known as the Dreaming Arm (Harrison 2001, p.28). The practitioner interrupts the client's expectation of what may occur by asking the question, 'May I borrow *that* arm ?'. By denoting the required arm as 'that', a sense of dissociation of ownership is induced; the arm is now an 'othered object' for the client. Lifting the arm into the air by placing a finger beneath the wrist, the practitioner states, 'I want your unconscious, now, to take control of that arm and hand, and I am not going to tell you lower that arm any faster than ...'.

At this point, a command is given by the practitioner, for example; 'you have him/her close their eyes and begin to relax more and more deeply ... and that arm and hand will only lower at the same pace with which you take him/her now into a deep state of comfort, peace and relaxation'.

This approach to therapeutic intervention is exemplified in the following case study:

Case Study Example: Two

A client, who for this paper shall be known as Amy, reported that she was so scared of the dental experience that she always had to undergo general sedation. This involved adjusting her diet the day before, taking two days off work; one for the dental visit and another to recover. Her husband also had to take a day off work to accompany and care for her.

I arranged to have a consultation with her on the morning of her next dental appointment. We spent a short time discussing the situation before guided her into a relaxed state. Once Amy was lightly relaxed, I performed the dreaming arm technique, instructing her unconscious to generate a new set of neuro associative responses at each stage of the dental experience; to have Amy's shoulders relax when she saw the outside of the dentist's building, and to have her internal narrative make an 'ahhhh', sound as she opened the door and smelt the interior of the waiting room. I also suggested that at the sound of the dentist drill, her unconscious take her into deepening states of peace, comfort and security, for this and every future dental experience. All of these transformational processes were to have been completed before her arm and hand had lowered and returned to their natural restful position.

The work was so successful that her dentist contacted me and asked if I would be willing to offer my services to other patients with similar fears. Amy's consultation took place in 1996, thirteen years before this paper was written and the results are still successful for her today. The following table shows how the therapeutic process of the NLP methodology used with Amy and Mary seems to correlate with the neuroscience discussed in this paper.

NLP and Neuroscience: Correlations

Stage	Stages of the therapeutic process, expressed in NLP terminology	Appears to correlate with	Stages of the therapeutic process, expressed in Neuroscience terminology
1	Rapport and Pace		Knowledge of Mirror Neurons used to induce relaxation and reduce resistance to change.
2	Relaxation and light trance		Initiation of the dissolution of unwanted neuro-pattern using metaphor and reframing while regulating the client's affect.
3	Ecology check		Creation of new synapse connections and neural pathways.
4	Dreaming Arm: Pattern Interrupt		Induction of pandemonium and creative environment and stimulation of affect.
5	Suggestions: commands for change		Re-direction of affect into new pathways, previously constructed during the ecology check.
6	Future Pace: Anchoring Establishment of new emotional responses		Neuro associative conditioning sustained with the cooperation of the amygdala and limbic system.

Case Study Example: Three

I would like to offer a third case example to illustrate how my learning from the AES course has changed my relationship with NLP. I have modified my working methods in a number of ways including changing the style of metaphorical approach from computing to neuroscience. Clients appear more willing to explore painful memories once the dynamics of affect regulation and the transformational alchemy of 'owning and yet containing' (Sasportas 1985, p 79) has been explained to them.

While undertaking the AES module, a new client began her therapeutic journey with me. At the age of thirty two she decided to resolve very serious issues from her childhood. Her extended family had recently discovered that she had been raped by her father and were reacting with powerful emotions. This had stirred up a host of repressed issues and memories for her, which now required urgent resolution. My knowledge of mirror neurons enabled me to more confidently pace and lead her into a relaxed state, reducing anxiety and easing her fears of exploring the past. I offered two metaphorical frameworks based on neuroscience and of the distinction between the sensation of affect and the meaning attributed to it; enabling her to reframe the emotion and its associated memories. Combining an understanding of the neuroscience of her experience with the application of NLP techniques meant she was able to self regulate the affective charge and modify subsequent emotion more easily (Fensbee 2007, p117). While her journey of transformation is not yet complete, being able to change her relationship with her history is enabling her to construct a new internal narrative in which she is the joyful participant of her present and the designer of her future, rather than the victim of a troubled past. On the day of writing the conclusion of this paper she was delighted to inform me that she had just become engaged.

Conclusion:

In this paper I have reflected on how being introduced to neuroscience on the AES programme has both informed and adapted my NLP practice. I have shown this by recounting my experience of being introduced to theories new to me and how these compare with NLP models of understanding language, memory and the process of change. Three case studies were presented to illustrate possible correlations between neuroscience and NLP perspectives.

While the scope of this formative paper is not that of a thorough investigation, it does suggest that there may be a basis in neuroscience for NLP. In addition, there may also be a place within NLP for neuroscience. There is most certainly a case for further research and development in this area, and it is my intention to use the findings gained from the research outlined in this paper as a platform upon which to conduct further study and investigation.

Bibliography:

Anxiety UK, formally the National Phobics Society: *Talking Therapies.*
http://www.anxietyuk.org.uk/talkingtherapies.php (sourced 12th
December 2008)

Bateman, Anthony and Holmes, Jeremy, *Introduction to Psychoanalysis,*
1995, Rotledge.

Bleandonu G, *Wilfred Bion: his life and his works 1897 – 1979,* 1994, Free
Association Books Ltd.

Callaghan Philip, *True Motivation : Creating a Personalised Propulsion
System,*
http://www.selfgrowth.com/articles/True_Motivation_Creating_a_Perso
nalised_Propulsion_System.html, sourced; 5th January 2009.

Cozolino, Louis, *The Neuroscience of Psychotherapy,* 2002, W. W. Norton.

Damasio Antonio, *The feeling of What Happens,* 2000, William
Heinerman.

Deleuze G, *Lecture Transcripts on Spinoza's Concept of Affect,*
http://www.goldsmiths.ac.uk/csisp/papers/deleuze_spinoza_affect.pdf,
sourced: 8th January 2009.
Dennet Daniel C., *Consciousness Explained,* 1993, Penguin Books Ltd.

Department of Health booklet 2008, *Choosing Talking Therapies,*
http://www.dh.gov.uk/en/Publicationsandstatistics/Publications/Publicati
onsPolicyAndGuidance/DH_4008162 (sourced 12th December 2008)

Edelman Gerald M. and Tononi Giulio, Consciousness: How matter
becomes imagination, 2000, Penguin Books Ltd.

Folensbee Rowland W, *The Neuroscience of Psychological Therapies,*
2007, Cambridge.

Fonagy Peter, Gergely Gyorgy, Jurist Elliot, Target Mary, *Affect Regulation,
Mentalization and the Development of the Self,* 2004, Other Press.

Harrison, M., *The Master Practitioner Suite Volumes One, Two and Three*, 2001, Tao Te Publishing.

Independent newspaper, http://www.guardian.co.uk/society/2006/mar/01/mentalhealth.socialcare1 (sourced 12th December 2008).

Indigo Eagle NLP Training, http://www.indigoeagle.com/index.php?page=whatisneurolinguisticprogramming, sourced: 4th January 2009.

Illingworth Nicola, 2001, *The Internet Matters: Exploring the Use of the Internet as a Research Tool Sociological Research Online,* vol. 6, no. 2, http://www.socresonline.org.uk/6/2/illingworth.html, sourced: 4th January 2009.

Mental Health Foundation. http://www.mentalhealth.org.uk/get-involved/donation/appeals/talking-therapies/ (sourced 12th December 2008)

Panksepp, Jaak, *Affective Consciousness*, in *The Blackwell Companion to Consciousness*, edited by Max Velmans and Susan Schneider, 2008, Blackwell Publishing Ltd.

Philips Helen, *Beautiful Minds*, featured in New Scientist magazine, 4th October 2008, Reed Business Information.

Pinker Steven, *The Stuff of Thought*, 2007, Penguin Books Ltd.

Resource Ecologies, http://www.resource-ecologies.co.uk/article_neuro.htm, sourced: 4th January 2009.
Rossi E. L., The Psychobiology of Mind-Body Healing, 1993, Norton.

Sasportas H, The Twelve Houses, 1985, Aquarian Press.

Schore Allen N., *Affect Regulation and the Origin of the Self*, 1994, Lawrence Erlbaum Associates.

Sport Health4u: Neuro Associative Conditioning,
http://www.sportshealth4u.com/nac.html (sourced 31st December 2008).

Stone Dr J, *Clinical Hypnotherapy; Improve your Health and Wealth*,
http://www.chicagohypnosis.info/NLPhypnosis.htm, sourced; 4th January
2009.

The Times,
http://women.timesonline.co.uk/tol/life_and_style/women/style/article7
21544.ece, sourced; 4th January 2008.

Wilkinson M, *Coming into Mind*, 2006, Routledge.

Forming an Attachment to Attachment Theory:

a journey to an emergent understanding.

Attachment theory addresses a universal human need to form close affectional bonds. A theory of both spatial and emotional proximity; with a cursory glance it may appear to be behavioural in principle. However, attachment theory has a basis in both ethology and evolutionary biology, incorporating systems of affect regulation and models of relational psychotherapy.

The approach I will take in this paper is that of recounting the formation of an understanding of attachment theory and my tentative explorations of applying some of its perspectives to cases from my client practice; both in the form of a historical review and then an account of an interview process, guided by the key principles of attachment theory as I understood them at that time. The journey of the paper will follow the same chronology as the salient landmarks of my learning process. I shall begin with an outline of my first encounter with attachment theory; a university lecture. A summary of my initial thoughts and intuitions will be followed by a deeper exploration of attachment theory.

A review of the supportive evidence from empirical studies and neuroscience will lay the foundation for the discussion of attachment theory. Relational perspectives will be explored, outlining both the schism between attachment theory and psychoanalysis and contemporary literature documenting the synthesis of their emergent integration. Four case studies will then be presented to demonstrate attachment theory in practice.

.

Hooked: an instant attachment to a guiding principle

As a student of psycho-social studies at the University of the West of England, I attended a lecture on attachment theory. It was given by a guest speaker, one of many who had, over a period of ten weeks, outlined a chronology of psychoanalytic psychotherapy in the British tradition. I was new to the subject and had no prior knowledge of attachment theory, or of the stature of the guest lecturer, Jeremy Holmes.

Holmes described the origins of attachment theory and how Bowlby felt that psychoanalytic thinking needed to be modified in the light of new evidence, especially from ethology (Bowlby, 1988, p.3). Although I found it interesting to hear of a psychotherapy model that has a basis in evolutionary theory (Craib, 2001, p.137), it was attachment theory's challenge to Freud's emphasis on sexuality which caught my interest (Holmes, 2001, p.24). It was largely because of Freud's models of sexual drives in infancy that I had been disinclined to enter the field of psychoanalytical psychotherapy. To be presented with a paradigm from psychotherapy which acknowledges the Oedipal triad and yet explains it not in terms of sexual drives but as an instinct for self protection and security, was illuminating and exciting (Mitchell, 2000. P.81). While I listened with one ear to an account of the secure base, relationships with attachment figures and modes of attachment behaviour, my attention was drawn into reviewing clients and personal experiences in a new light; my attention was hooked.

Key principles that remain with me from the lecture:

- Ethology studies have shown the need for a secure base is ubiquitous in nature. (Bowlby, 1988, p.33).

- A secure base acts like the sanctuary from which explorations into the world can be launched and into which one can return for safety (Bowlby, 1979, p.125).

- All affectionate bonds are ruptured during the course of ordinary living (Bowlby, 1979, p.86). It is the quality of reparation, satisfactory or otherwise, which forms the basis of a particular style of response to anxiety when security is threatened (Cozolino, 2006, p. 140). These responsive styles are known as attachment behaviours (Bowlby, 1988, p.31).

- There are three main types of behaviour triggered by the arousal of the attachment system, one of which may be viewed in polarity (Cozolino, 2006, p. 141). These will be further discussed in more detail.

a) Secure Attachment

b) Insecure attachment type one: Avoidant Attachment

c) Insecure Attachment type two: Ambivalent Attachment

d) Disorganised Attachment

- When activated, patterns of attachment are accompanied by an arousal of affect (Schore, 1994, p.387), reparation, or soothing, aids in the regulation of affect (Fonagay et al. 2004, p37).

- Activation of attachment behaviour prompts a desire to seek and return to the secure base with immediate effect (Craib, 2001, p. 137). In adult life, different people may act as attachment figures (Holmes, 2001, p.29). Holmes advised that, in therapeutic practice, asking a client who to call in case of emergency will reveal the identity of their current attachment figure.

- The psychotherapeutic consultation may come to constitute a secure base (Holmes, 1996, p.123), its enduring consistency facilitating a regulation of affect (Schore, 2003, p.262) which, if internalised, becomes affective self regulation from the position of the secure base (Fonagay et al., 2004, p.435).

My initial thoughts after the lecture were that attachment theory made clear sense. It addressed a personal challenge with Freud's sexual theories, had a firm basis in evolutionary theory and related to another study I was undertaking regarding affect and affect regulation. I found myself thinking of human history with an anthropological perspective; images of the upper primates holding on in the canopy, high above the ground came to mind. To fall may not only be dangerous; one may become lost from the group. My enthusiasm for the topic found expression with an intensity that was obvious to another student. The irruptive affect signified that I had already begun to form a relational bond with attachment theory and I made the instantaneous decision to conduct this investigation.

From apprehension to comprehension: the formation of a deeper understanding.

The concept of attachment can be viewed in two ways. A prefatory attempt to grasp what may be meant by the term, attachment theory, may prompt an instinctive and reductive conclusion that it refers to matters of being attached. When I first heard the term, *Attachment Theory*, my initial thoughts were of having a familiarity with the concept of being attached to things or objects; people, memories, places, routines and habits. However, further investigation revealed an approach to understanding human behaviour which has a basis in evolutionary biology, relational psychotherapy and neuroscience.

Attachment theory is more than a theory of behavioural typology. It is also a control systems theory which has a dynamic quality at it core. Kirkpatrick writes, 'the system is organized to activate a particular behaviour or suite of behaviours whenever a stimulus appears' (Kirkpatrick, 2005, p.28). A vulnerable infant maintains security by remaining in close proximity to care givers. In *The Search for the Secure Base*, Holmes writes:

> The vulnerable newborn infant on the ancestral savannah needed to ensure proximity to care-givers if he was to be safe from predation. The mother-infant attachment responses (i.e. distress calls and proximity-seeking) keep him safe from macro-predation and help regulate his emotional states, just as the antibody-rich colostrum she provides keeps micro-organisms at bay. (Holmes, 2001, p.1).

Shore reports that the dyadic interaction between the newborn and primary carer modulates and controls the infant's homeostasis and that, '... attachment theory is fundamentally a regulatory theory' (Shore, 2003, p118). Cozolino asserts that, 'attachment schemas reflect the transduction of interpersonal experience into the biological structure', the dynamics of the affective experience correlate with linkages of the orbital medial prefrontal cortex and the amygdala with the regulatory systems (Cozolino, 2006, p. 146).

Shore's earlier findings show that the psychobiological attunement of attachment occurs in relationships throughout the lifespan. The operation of the attachment dynamic continues to occur in adult life and the activation of an internal system, first developed with the primary carer, maintains an affective state of enjoyment and well being (Shore, 1994, p107).

It may be unwise to think of this regulatory system as akin to that of a thermostat control, because the attachment system has a variable fixed point. In a thermostat, the temperature is compared to the point set and then temperature is adjusted accordingly. In contrast, the desired level of proximity in which a sense of security is engendered may vary according to circumstance, ranging from being tightly held to out of sight (Kirkpatrick, 2005, p. 29). Bowlby speaks of the fear response that may be stimulated not only because of a high risk of pain or danger, but also because of an increase of risk (Bowlby, 1988, p. 33). Environmental factors such as unfamiliarity, isolation, heights, looming objects and sudden loud noises activate the fear and attachment system. The attachment behaviours, such as crying, are designed to bring an attachment figure into closer proximity. If successful, the system is deactivated. The seeking of a secure base may be complimented with other systems vital to secure development and learning; exploration and the fear (Kirkpatrick, 2005, p. 30). A relational and autopoietic (Capra, 1996, p.97) control system, comprising attachment, exploration and fear, regulates and guides the ongoing safety and continued development of an individual via a means of activation, or deactivation of these interdependent systems (Fonagay, 2001, p. 9).

The deactivation of affective arousal can be mediated by reunion with an attachment figure, most usually the mother. Shore attests that reunion behaviour is more indicative of the quality of attachment than, for example, a child's protests at a point of separation (Shore, 1994, p.100). Bion postulated the maternal container, whose capacity for reverie transforms the unpleasant sensations (Fonagat et al, 2004, p. 191). Reunion transactions with the attuned care giver maintain the arousal level; an infant's reentering into patterned interactive states with the care giver regulates the arousal, affective and attention state of the infant. This is mediated by visual contact with the mother, or care giver.

46

Shore proposes a visuoaffective transaction during which, 'the mother's facially expressed emotional communications provide the infant with salient maternal appraisals of interactions and events (Shore, 1994, p.100). Kirkpatrick reports there are parallels between infant-mother interactions and those between adult lovers; prolonged eye contact, cooing or talking "baby talk," and other intimate behaviors are similar to those displayed by infants to elicit and maintain contact with an attachment figure (Kirkpatrick, 2005 p 40).

Psychoanalytic perspectives.

Conceptual differences that once divided the psychoanalytic and attachment traditions have begun to find common ground in relationality (Mitchell, 2000. P. 83). The internal focus of early psychotherapy; drives, instincts and fantasy, are seemingly at odds with attachment theory's apparent mechanistic and behavioural emphasis (Criab, 2001, p. 141). Relational theorists such as Sullivan, '... portrayed the early interactions between the infant and its human environment as shaping an almost infinitely malleable collection of human potentials to fit an interpersonal niche to which that potential becomes finely adapted.' (Fonagay, 2001, p.126). In his conclusion on attachment and relationality, Mitchell writes, '...the apparent separation between the subject who attaches and the object of attachment overlays a primary process level of organization in which self and other exist in various degrees of undifferentiating from each other.' (Mitchell, 2000. P. 101). He concludes, '... healthy object relations (and by implication, healthy attachments) consist not so much in a clear separation of self from others, but in a capacity to contain in dialectical tensions different mutually enriching forms of relatedness.' (Mitchell, 2000. P. 101).

Another development in psychoanalytic thought that enables attachment theory to find commonality with psychotherapy is mentalization. Showing the relationship between affect regulation and mentalization, Fonagay et al. suggest a theory of mentalized affectivity in which affects are used to regulate the self and that mentalized affectivity lies at the core of psychotherapy. (Fonagay et al, 2004, p.5). They postulate:

> Our theory of affect regulation and mentalization
> enables us to enrich the arguments advanced by
> theorists such as John Bowlby about the evolutionary
> function of attachment. We argue that an evolutionary
> function of early object relations is to equip the very
> young child with an environment within which the
> understanding of mental states in others and the self
> can fully develop. We propose that self-reflection as
> well as the ability to reflect on other minds are
> constructed capacities that have evolved (or not) out of

the earliest relationships. Since mentalization is a core aspect of human social functioning, we can infer that evolution has placed particular value on developing mental structures for interpreting interpersonal actions. (Fonagay et al, 2004, p.5).

Attachment systems.

Because attachment behaviour patterns operate on an unconscious level, they continue to function throughout the life span and are known as the Internal Working Models (Holmes, 2001, p 29). In his biographical work, *John Bowlby and Attachment Theory*, Holmes writes:

> Bowlby wished to recast psychoanalytic theory in terms of a systems approach in which feedback loops are a key element, they underlie the 'epigenetic' stability of psychological phenomena: the benign circles of healthy development, and the vicious circles of neurosis in which negative assumptions about the self and others become self-fulfilling prophecies. (Holmes, 1993, p.79).

Contemporary attachment theorists such as Ainsworth and Main have placed an emphasis not on the typology of attachment behaviour but on the degree of coherence, or incoherence in the subject's account of childhood memories (Mitchell, 2000, p.85). Ainsworth conducted research known as the strange situation in which a child's reaction to brief separation was observed (Holmes, 2001, p. 33). The Adult Attachment Interview (AAI) is foremost among the methods used to assess the propensity to activate attachment systems in adults. The interview takes the form of eliciting from the subject a narrative of their childhood with the therapist's attention being given to coherence and quality of the client's expression. The narrative styles are coded: 'Attachment security in the coding system (the autonomous classification—F) is most closely associated with high coherence. There are three insecure patterns: the dismissing (idealizing or derogatory about attachment—Ds), the preoccupied (angry or passive—E), and the unresolved in relation to loss or abuse (U)'. (Fonagay, 2001, p.23).

In the *Search for a Secure Base*, Holmes presents a table correlating child and adult attachment patterns (Holmes, 2001, p.38). This can be seen in Appendix 1.

Kirkpatrick describes findings from his own research regarding attachment patterns in adult relationships:

1. *Avoidant:* I am somewhat uncomfortable being close to others; I find it difficult to trust them completely, difficult to allow myself to depend on them. I am nervous whenever anyone gets too close, and often, others want me to be more intimate than I feel comfortable being.

2. *Secure:* I find it relatively easy to get close to others and am comfortable depending on them and having them depend on me. I don't worry about being abandoned or about someone getting too close to me.

3. *Anxious/ambivalent:* I find that others are reluctant to get as close as I would like. I often worry that my partner doesn't really love me or won't want to stay with me. I want to get very close to my partner, and this sometimes scares people away (Kirkpatrick, 2005 p 40).

With regard to adult relationships, Bateman and Holmes also report:

Secure attachment provides a positive primary defense while secondary or pathological defenses retain closeness to rejecting or unreliable attachment figures. In 'avoidant attachment', both neediness and aggression are split off and the individual has no conscious knowledge of the need to be near the attachment figure, appearing aloof and distant; in 'ambivalent attachment', omnipotence and denial of autonomy lead to clinging and uncontrolled demands. (Bateman & Holmes, 1995, p. 78)

Patterns of attachment are not typological and are useful guides to assessing the present state of condition of an individual. In practice, clients show both ambivalent and avoidant patterns at different times and according to context (Holmes, 2001, p.28).

Throughout the life span, attachment systems may be activated by threats to security. A variety of things may represent a secure base for an individual, the most obvious being a parent or romantic partner. In addition to therapists, other care workers such as hospital staff can become surrogate attachment figures and non-clinical adults have been known to describe their secure base as pets, family, close friends, hot baths, duvets, photograph albums, being in touch with nature, favourite books and music (Holmes, 2001, p 29). Kirkpatrick reports from his research into the psychology of religions that not just religious figures and leaders, but also God may become a secure base (Kirkpatrick, 2005, p.65). Mental health bodies advise, 'a stable routine and structure at home will provide a secure base for your child', (Collingwood, J., 2009), implying that anticipatory time-bound structures may also signify security for an individual.

Attachment theory in practice.

For this study I propose to examine four case studies at varying depths of complexity.

During the lecture when I was introduced to attachment theory, I identified four people from my client history who I thought may be suitable for investigation. The set of four comprised two men and two women. For the purpose of this study, I decided to give them pseudonyms, in order to protect their identity: Amber and Jade, Ash and Dylan.

On the surface the two men seemed to have no common ground, while the two women shared a number of common factors. Both women had been sexually abused by family members when young. Both are in their thirties and neither has yet become a parent. There were a number of contrasting factors which prompted my decision to include them in the study: both women were born in England and yet one had a British-Asian background. Amber, the British-Asian woman had a Muslim family background while Jade's background was heavily influenced by the tenets of astrological and esoteric philosophy. Jade was a smoker who enjoyed drinking; Amber had never drank alcohol in her life and had only tried a cigarette as a youthful experiment. Both worked in finance, though while Jade was untrained and sustained a medium to low level accounting career, Amber was highly ambitious, driven and had taken senior management roles in global household name companies. Although neither were parents, Jade had taken up the position of caring for a partner's children on occasion, while Amber had chosen a husband who could not have children. While neither of their partners had become financially successful, it is interesting to note that Jade, the woman who appears to lack ambition, has a partner whose income is in close proximity to hers. This is in contrast with Amber, the successful woman's husband had an income that measured barely 15% of hers; this may suggest that proportionate and disproportionate economic responsibility may have a bearing on matters of control and security.

On the surface, the two men appear to be very different. Ash is in his early forties, has been married for five years, has a son of eleven and currently lives in South Africa. Originally from Kenya, he has also lived in

England. Dylan is also in his early forties, has lived his life either in, or in close proximity to the English village of his childhood. He is a divorcee with no children. Further differences are evident; Dylan went to school in his village, Ash was sent to boarding school at the age of seven. Ash has had a number of jobs and has recently found his vocation as a qualified acupuncturist. Dylan has remained in the same warehouse job for more than twenty five years.

Ash.

A view from the surface: Attachment to:

In terms of looking at attachment, Ash appears to have a pattern that is ubiquitous. He was close to his parents but when they argued, he would keep his distance, waiting for their cue that they had repaired their bond. Being sent away to boarding school was unbearable for Ash. Once more he found he had to wait for external or environmental cues, namely, school   holidays, to have permission to repair the bonds with his parents and return to the secure base of the family home. The enforced exclusion from his secure base appears to have constellated a pattern akin to attachment-elastic, in which Ash is in a constant state of transitioning convergence and divergence with things that represent powerful attachments in his life.

In his youth, Ash became a member of a martial arts training club which, in his words, was like a cult. It was here that he met his wife, daughter of the martial arts leader and a period began in which they were together but not free to live as they wished; many of their decisions were at the behest of the will of the group, the leader or at times, the leader's new partner. The strain on their marriage was too much and they parted temporarily. His wife came to the UK and a short while later they repaired their relationship and he joined her in Britain. Seven years later, his wife decided to return to South Africa to be near her now divorced father. Once again Ash was uncertain whether to break up or follow and he decided to return to South Africa with his wife. Within a year she had met someone who reminded her of the thrills of blossoming romance on a course she attended in the UK, while Ash remained in South Africa, and subsequently found himself spending the next twelve months waiting for his wife to decide whether she wanted to stay or leave.

During our discussion on attachments, Ash informed me he had a passion for motorbikes and had been a smoker, both of these were experienced as an on-off dynamic.

On the surface it would appear that Ash has an anxious/ambivalent relationship with attachment.

Beneath the surface: Attachment dynamics:

Since 2007, Ash has been engaged in an almost constant process of reviewing his history and seeking reparation and resolution. When recounting early childhood experiences, his voice was sometimes be hesitant, occasionally stuttering. His present preoccupation with reviewing his history enabled him to construct a cohesive narrative and when asked about an area that has received previous consideration his manner was clear, concise and articulate, though affect appeared subdued.

My conclusion is that Ash is making a transition from Ambivalent to Secure attachment.

Dylan:

A view from the surface: Attachment to:

A word that I would use describe Dylan is consistent. Others may opt for the word secure, but I think even at the surface, this would be an error. Dylan has no desire to change his job or to seek promotion within the company. At the age of forty he found himself living on his own, in his own house, with no outstanding mortgage. He has only had one partner in life; his wife of seven years who he divorced four years ago. Much of his life appears to revolve around his family. His choice of car is influenced by familial needs and wishes, the weekly routine is constant, with Sunday lunch being an event unchanged since his childhood. There is certainly a lack of exploration in his life; even when having broadband installed in his home after fourteen months of consumer assessment; it remained unused for two months after purchase. Dylan appears to manage his life on a continuum of maintaining sameness. He also demonstrates obsessive compulsive disorder behaviours, which remain without formal diagnosis or therapeutic treatment. He was bullied at school, and this ecxpereince was repeated in his only adult relationship. An incident of rejection at the age of seventeen is a salient feature of his narrative and supports his present orientation of giving more value to avoiding the risks of rejection than forming affectional bonds with an adult and his own offspring. He reports that he is concerned about expression of his temper, preferring to maintain consistently passive. He appears to self consciously attend to regulating his affect in the company of others.

On the surface it would appear that Dylan has an avoidant attachment style.

Beneath the surface: Attachment dynamics:

When recounting his past, Dylan maintains a subdued affect, normalising his history and is seemingly uninterested in any form of therapeutic resolution of historical issues which continue to cause him either distress or influence current life experience. Dylan is hesitant to begin talking, but once underway, he expresses himself with an easy disposition and good humour. On the surface Dylan is a paradox; a secure man with no attachments. Beneath the surface, a maintenance of distance, controlled affect and disinterest in actively resolving issues and bringing positive change into his life, confirm that Dylan has an avoidant attachment style.

Jade:

A view from the surface: Attachment to:

At the age of thirty three, Jade is navigating the waters of recovery from severe sexual abuse. Her family home was peaceful while her father worked away, but his return would precipitate an atmosphere of anxiety, if not fear itself. Her father was a controlling man, oriented around work and material success. In contrast, Jade's mother was peaceful, and spiritually orientated and had no awareness that Jade was raped by her father. This occurred on more than one occasion before Jade was five years old. She seemed uncertain about recounting when it came to an end; the details were, understandably, hesitant and vague. Jade's parents separated when she was around ten years old. Jade later went to boarding school and reports deriving a sense of both exploratory escape and self searching and a denying of a sense of abandonment or rejection. Through her adult life Jade has formed relationships consistent with healthy youth. Long term attachments have endured for approximately three years. Since embarking on her journey of therapy, Jade has made remarkable changes. She had kept her abuse a secret, shared only with her mother and brother. Recently, her brother angrily let the secret out at a family gathering and a schism resulted. In a manner akin to structural coupling (Capra, 1996, p.213), the rupture to the family security has led to sides being taken with calls for a legal prosecution in order to have her account verified. The group dynamic is a response reminiscent of the ambivalent attachment pattern; the family want to know and yet hate having to know, and the suppressed affect is directed as anger towards Jade. These events have proved to be a catalyst for her in a number of ways: she has embarked on a course of professional training, stepping out from her avoidance of heightened material success. She has become engaged, has stopped smoking and displays a greater sense of self confidence.

On the surface, it would appear that Jade has an ambivalent attachment style.

Beneath the surface: Attachment dynamics:

Jade has a voice that resonates with clear ringing tones and an articulate manner of expression. Occasional waves of affect surface though her general communications, which serve to bring a lively effervescence to her social interaction. During therapy, her manner remains the same until historical narrative is investigated. She appears to shift from curiosity to uncertainty, hesitant to explore her feelings and yet feels compelled to do so.

A salient feature of Jade's narrative was the distress she still experienced from being unable to remove an image of the look on her father's face, prevalent during his raping of her. The affect transformation was intense and it was decided to apply a hypnotic technique from the field of neuro linguistic programming to enable her to reconfigure the memory and deactivate the aroused affect. The intervention proved successful and Jade reported she was no longer haunted by the image.

The therapeutic journey Jade has undertaken is incubating reparation and enabling her to establish relationships with both others and herself which are life affirming and supportive. Reviewing Jade's present position, I draw the conclusion that she is making a transition from an ambivalent attachment system to security.

Amber:

A view from the surface: Attachment to:

Amber embarked on a therapeutic journey that has taken a variety of forms around the time of her thirtieth birthday. She had a history of severe, regular and systematic sexual abuse from more than one family member, which began when she was four years old. The perpetrators were brothers and she was also abused by a religious leader in a Mosque. She reported that abuse from males seemed ubiquitous though did this not include her father, who constituted a secure base. Amber was fostered at birth for six months and, she reports, formed an affectionate bond with her foster parents. The degree of affection was absent in her relationship with her mother, who seemed detached and cold, preoccupied with her own concerns and maintaining the reputation of the family name within the culture. Not all of her brothers were abusive, though the ones who were took it in turns. Amber would often hide in cupboards or under the bed to escape; when escape was not possible, she would retreat into a world of television and books. In addition to sexual abuse there was a high level of aggression in family communication and bullying in other forms. At eight years of age, Amber told her mother of the abuse after maintaining secrecy for four years, only to be shunned and called a 'whore'. The death of Amber's father when she was fourteen engendered an urgent need in her to assert herself as a matter of self defence and she embarked upon a path of focussed determination to make self reliant progress in life. By the time of her thirtieth birthday Amber had completed a twelve year programme of self-taught study and qualified as an accountant. Professional success was the focus of her life. Romantic attachments were infrequent, comprising two to three years in duration. It was during her thirtieth year that she met her husband. She had an image of a successful, professional life partner and chose instead a man who, while soft, kind and compassionate, lacked material success, was unable to produce children and as an adult with aspergers syndrome, is himself in need of care. Amber, in the search for a secure base, chose a husband with whom she could represent a figure of secure attachment. An uneasy alliance has grown into a secure companionship which she has now been able to maintain for ten years. During this time she has undertaken additional training in NLP and hypnotherapy, interior design and yoga. She is currently a participant in a two year course in Buddhism and has been accepted for an MSc in economics.

Amber's journey has taken many steps towards recovery and is ongoing. In 2002, after a period of counselling, she reached a stage of drawing a line beneath her past and she reported her abuse to the police. Although Amber refrained from proceeding to prosecution, this still caused a major rift between the women of the family; Amber, her mother and elder sister. She began a process of cautious reparation in 2006.

During the course of our discussions on attachments, she experienced an overpowering affective response which precipitated the recovery of an amygdala based memory of the very moment when her abuse began. She had previously known of this event, in a vague and intellectual way, but this was her first experience of full comprehension.

As a result of the emotional recovery, Amber has reported that she feels differently towards her past and her abusers. Significantly, the hunger to be accepted and loved by those who hurt has ceased, as if it had melted away. She speaks with a renewed sense of vision and appreciation for the attachments which constitute a secure base in her life.

Amber's attachment pattern has changed over a long period of time. When I first encountered her, she was an adult, afraid of the dark and displayed powerful disorganised attachment behaviour combined with avoidance. At present, she is apt to display a lesser degree of ambivalent attachment.

Beneath the surface: Attachment dynamics:

The improved coherence of Amber's narrative signifies a continuing progress and marks a transition from disorganised attachment towards security via avoidance and ambivalence. The matter of her maternity has yet to be resolved and remains a thorny issue. She does report, however, that her recovery from her childhood is steadily progressing and the improved clarity in her narrative and comprehension suggest this is definitely the case.

I would conclude that Amber is establishing an internal secure base.

Conclusion:

This paper has given an account of my relationship with attachment theory. I have described my initial encounter with the theory during a lecture; given a review of the supportive literature and also given a report of my findings when the theory is applied in practice.

I was somewhat reticent towards the idea of applying set patterns or working models towards an individual, preferring instead to relate with a client's unique experience. However, I have been surprised at how closely the descriptions of attachment patterns apply to the cases in this paper. This formative study serves as an introduction to attachment theory and I intend to conduct further research in this area.

Attachment perspectives have already begun to inform a greater degree of perception in my own client practice and I have certainly begun to form an attachment to attachment theory.

Bibliography.

Bateman, Anthony and Holmes, Jeremy, 1995, *Introduction to Psychoanalysis*, Routledge.

Bowlby, 1979, *The Making and Breaking of Affectional Bonds*, Routeledge.

Bowlby, 1988, *A Secure Base*, Routeledge.

Capra, F, 1996, The Web of Life, Harper Collins.

Collingwood, J., *Helping a Family Member with a Mental Disorder*, http://psychcentral.com/lib/2006/helping-a-family-member-with-a-mental-disorder/

Cozolino, L, 2006, *The Neuroscience of Human Relationships*, W. W. Norton and Company

Craib, I., 2001, *Psychoanalysis: a critical introduction*, Polity Press.

Fonagay, P., 2001, *Attachment Theory and Psychoanalysis*, Karnac Books.

Fonagay, P., Gergely, G., Jurist, E., Target, M., 2004, *Affect Regulation, Mentalization, and the Development of the Self*, Other Press.

Holmes, J., 1993, *John Bowlby and Attachment Theory*, Routeledge.

Holmes, J., 1996, *Attachment, Intimacy, Autonomy.*, Aronson.

Holmes, 2001, *The Search for the Secure Base*, Routeledge.

Kirkpatrick, L. A., 2005, *Attachment, Evolution and the Psychology of Religion*, The Guildford Press.

Mitchell, S. A., 2000, *Relationality: From Attachment to Intersubjectivity*, The Analytic Press.

Schore, A., 1994, *Affect Regulation and Origin of the Self*, Lawrence Erlbaum Associates Inc.

Schore, A., 2003, *Affect Regulation and the Repair of the Self*, W. W. Norton and Company.

Appendix 1.

Table 2.1 Adult Attachment Interview classifications and corresponding patterns of infant strange situation behaviour

Adult state of mind with respect to attachment	Infant strange situation behaviour
Secure/autonomous (F) Coherent, collaborative discourse. Valuing of attachment, but seems objective regarding any particular event or relationship. Description and evaluation of attachment-related experiences is consistent, whether experiences are favourable or unfavourable. Discourse does not notably violate any of Grice's maxims	**Secure (B)** Explores room and toys with interest in pre-separation episodes. Shows signs of missing parent during separation, often crying by the second separation. Obvious preference for parent over stranger. Greets parent actively, usually initiating physical contact. Usually some contact maintained by second reunion, but then settles and returns to play
Dismissing (Ds) Not coherent. Dismissing of attachment-related experiences and relationships. Normalizing ('excellent, very normal mother'), with generalized representations of history unsupported or actively contradicted by episodes recounted, thus violating Grice's maxim of quality. Transcripts also tend to be excessively brief, violating the maxim of quantity	**Avoidant (A)** Fails to cry on separation from parent. Actively avoids and ignores parent on reunion (i.e. by moving away, turning away or leaning out of arms when picked up). Little or no proximity or contact-seeking, no distress and no anger. Response to parent appears unemotional. Focuses on toys or environment throughout procedure
Preoccupied (E) Not coherent. Preoccupied with or by past attachment relationships or experiences, speaker appears angry, passive or fearful. Sentences often long, grammatically entangled, or filled with vague usages ('dadadada', 'and that'), thus violating Grice's maxims of manner and relevance. Transcripts often excessively long, violating the maxim of quantity	**Resistant or ambivalent (C)** May be wary or distressed even before separation, with little exploration. Preoccupied with parent throughout procedure; may appear angry or passive. Fails to settle and take comfort in parent on reunion, and usually continues to focus on parent and cry. Fails to return to exploration after reunion
Unresolved/disorganized (U) During discussions of loss or abuse, individual shows striking lapse in the monitoring of reasoning or discourse. For example, individual may briefly indicate a belief that a dead person is still alive in the physical sense, or that this person was killed by a childhood thought. Individual may lapse into prolonged silence or eulogistic speech. The speaker will ordinarily otherwise fit Ds, E or F categories	**Disorganized /disoriented (D)** The infant displays disorganized and/or disoriented behaviours in the parent's presence, suggesting a temporary collapse of behavioural strategy. For example, the infant may freeze with a trance-like expression, hands in air; may rise at parent's entrance, then fall prone and huddled on the floor; or may cling while crying hard and leaning away with gaze averted. Infant will ordinarily otherwise fit A, B or C categories

Sources: Adapted from Hesse (1999).

Notes: Descriptions of the adult attachment classification system are summarized from Main *et al.* (1985) and from Main and Goldwyn (1984a, 1998a). Descriptions of infant A, B and C categories are summarized from Ainsworth *et al.* (1978) and the description of the infant D category is summarized from Main and Solomon (1990). Data from Main (1996).

A Place to belong:

investigating the relationship between landscape and identity

A pilot study in Psycho-Social research exploring the dynamics of two faith groups in an English village, situated within a World Heritage Site.

It is a mark of human nature that mankind impresses his identity onto the landscape. This is a pilot study investigating the relationship between landscape and environment from a psycho-social perspective. Society fashions the landscape that surrounds it but does the landscape also inform and colour the identity of both society and individuals? Object relations theory may suggest the inner landscape of the psyche is influenced by the external landscape; what is the relationship between identity and landscape?

This paper is also a field study. Exploring the relationship between the inner and outer dynamics of the individual and landscape, of society and identity, requires a methodology that extends beyond conventional social science and personal psychotherapy. The emerging field of Psycho-Social Studies indicates that the foundations of a methodology have already been laid, and in this respect, this paper has a dual purpose; to investigate both the relationship between identity and landscape and to also conduct an exploratory review of Psycho-Social research methods in practice.

Initially, the paper will give a background to the context and focus of the study and describe its original intention. It will then review psycho-social perspectives and the research methodology used for this study before proceeding to the research itself. I will show from the reflexive analysis how the dynamics of the research can be explored at a much deeper level than merely reporting what is presented on the surface. The orientation, or identity, of the paper itself changes when emergent themes were revealed in direct response to application of psycho-social methodology in practice. The paper will describe the process of uncovering the unconscious material and explore both the value and potential for further study of this topic using psycho-social research methodology.

Avebury: history and society in its place.

This formative paper is the first step in an investigation of the reparative dynamics of the Stonehenge Truth and Reconciliation Committee (TRC), based upon the TRC in post Apartheid South Africa.

On the 1st of June 1985 a severe civil disturbance, known as the 'Battle of the Beanfield' (Hawkes, 2009), near the site of Stonehenge bought a temporary end to the use of Stonehenge as a temple of worship for Druids and other Pagan interest groups. There were scenes of unrest at the site for a number of years to the dissatisfaction of all parties concerned, mainly; Druid and Pagan groups, the police, local farmers and land owners, English Heritage. The Stonehenge TRC was instigated and conducted over a period of time, giving a voice and sense of value to all of the groups represented. This culminated in the restoration of the temple being opened for Solstice worship in the year 2000. It is reported that in excess of thirty thousand people attend the summer solstice celebrations at Stonehenge and have done so peacefully for the past nine years (BBC, 2008).

As a prelude towards this future study, this pilot study in psycho-social research investigates the dynamics between the two significant faith groups in Avebury. Avebury is a place of duality; it is both a traditional English village and a World Heritage Neolithic monument; the largest stone circle in Europe. Construction of the site began c 3000BCE (English Heritage, 2009), while other significant archaeological sites such as round barrows, long barrows, hill forts and Silbury Hill, that comprise and give shape to the ancient Avebury landscape were constructed over a period of time from c 3500 BCE until the Iron Age. The Neolithic population that constructed Avebury Henge had left the area without any trace before the Celtic Druid priesthood had come to Britain. Hutton reports that there is only one reference in literature in which the Druids, 'are actually portrayed in Britain (or at least right next to it)', (Hutton, 2007, p.3). In the early 60s CE the Romans massacred the Druids on the island of Anglesey, virtually ending Druidism in Britain. The first modern Druid order was founded in 1772 (Hutton, 2007, p.21). Avebury village first appeared between 500-600 CE as a Saxon settlement (Panayi, 2009), and an early wooden Saxon church was constructed c 1000 CE (Wiltshire Council, 2009) . From the time of its construction Avebury remained virtually untouched until two destructions took place; the first in 1320 CE, followed by a period of destruction during the eighteenth and nineteenth centuries (Wheatley & Taylor, 2008, p.7). In the 1930s, an archaeologist and marmalade millionaire, Alexander Keiller, bought Avebury and much of its surrounding landscape. A period of restoration began which continued after World War two.

Avebury is in a unique position; it is a small village set within an ancient stone circle. The community is comprised of secular elements and followers of various religions, the most visible of which are Christianity and Paganism. The church spire dominates the village and from each road approaching Avebury, huge sarsen stones stand like sentinel gate keepers. The church spire is an obvious religious icon, impressing its identity onto the village, while the Pagan presence is more subtle, made visible by the occasional gathering of Druids or other Pagans. Avebury is also a World Heritage site and is periodically host to thousands of visitors who also comprise of secular tourists, Pagan worshipers, Christian tourists, archaeologists, authors and media and university researchers.

The original intent of this paper was to explore psycho-social methodology by investigating the interrelational dynamics between the two most visible faith groups in Avebury; the Druids and the Christians. In the planning stage of this paper, Avebury was seen as nothing more than a small container for a micro-study of group dynamics. I was intrigued to discover how tolerances were managed and to what extent any issues of overt prejudice, transference or projective identification may be evident. Another possible line of enquiry was that of ownership; do either of the faith groups lay claim to being, or unconsciously behave as if they are the rightful inheritors of Avebury as a place of worship?

The Christians may face criticism that the temple has been ruined with their destruction of the stones, but Christianity is recognised in law. The Pagans and Druids have no legal position, and yet they may argue that Avebury is a pre-Christian temple and so it is their rightful place. As previously mentioned, Avebury is Neolithic in origin and all of the faith groups present have migrated into a landscape that was fashioned long before their arrival.

Researching beneath the surface: an overview of Psycho-Social research methodologies and approaches.

In *Object relations and social relations*, Susie Orbach writes;

> The understanding of relational analysis starts
> from the premise that the individual is born into a
> set of social and psychological circumstances. The
> human infant is *a set of possibilities,* not id based, not
> instinctually driven, but, in order to become
> recognized as human, will need to attach. For those
> compelled by the notion of instinct theory, this was
> reframed in the 1940s by Fairbairn as a need for
> relationship, and by Bowlby as a need for attachment.
> The nature of the relationships the child is exposed to,
> experiences, and, of course, seeks to shape by her
> actions, is the template for that individual's self
> experience and relations to others. Relational psycho-
> analysis does not seek to understand the structures
> in a reductionist way, or by use of sociological tools.
> Its agenda is to understand how both the satisfactory
> and the problematic aspects of those profoundly
> influential relationships create the internal
> structuring of the individual. (Orbach, 2008, p 31)

Hoggett elaborates further, describing the relational turn in psychoanalysis as an approach which can, 'grasp the continued interplay between the real and the imagined', (Hoggett, 2008 p.73). A narrative style interview in which open questions are employed (Clarke, 2008 p.121) creates a relationship with the subject which allows a gestalt to emerge (Hollway & Jefferson, 2000, p.40). A similar approach is employed in the field of neuro linguistic programming (NLP) (Bandler and Grinder, 1975 p.41). The NLP model suggests that to begin a question with the word 'why', prompts the recipient to respond in a defensive manner and a search for justification will be initiated. The question, 'why ?' tends to stimulate the answer, 'because ...' and the recipient delivers a justification. However, if a question begins with the word, 'what ...?' it initiates a search for content, while 'how ... ?' stimulates an inner search for the process of something. 'who ...?' addresses the performer; who is present, or absent, while 'where ... ?', can generate a quest to determine either a geographical place or a place within time, which may also be sought by asking, 'when ... ?' (Harrison 2001, p.205).

An ontological approach towards identity and positioning (Hollway, 2008, p.141) that is both intrapsychic and interpsychic gives a renewed value to the subjective interpretation of narrative in research. Reminiscent of Ogden's Third Way (Ogden, 1999, p.109), in *the epistemology of testimony*, Jennifer Lackey speaks of the dual nature of testimony; where both the speaker's and listener's condition play an equal role in the epistemic value of the material (Lackey & Sosa, 2006, p.170).

Wendy Hollway writes:

> Bion's concept of the container-contained relationship affords a powerful tool for understanding both intersubjectivity and individuality and provides a radical foundation for a psycho-social research epistemology. We learn through identifications with objects. This is at the core of the idea that researchers can use their subjectivity as an instrument of knowing (Hollway, 2008, p.149).

Using the researcher's subjectivity as a research tool is controversial (Hollway,2008, p.156). However, of the three approaches to counter-transference outlined by Laplanche and Pontalis, two are of value to the psycho-social researcher. The recognition by Freud that, 'everyone possesses in his own unconscious an instrument with which he can interpret the utterances of the unconscious in other people', (Freud, 1931, cited in Laplanceh & Pontalis, 1973) is supportive of the psycho-social method. However, Laplanche and Pontalis offer further comment;

... to allow oneself to be guided, in the actual *interpretation,* by one's own counter-transference reactions, which in this perspective are often not distinguished from emotions felt. This approach is based on the tenet that resonance 'from unconscious to unconscious' constitutes the only authentically psycho-analytic form of communication (Laplanche & Pontalis, 1973, p93).

Bion's notion of reverie; a frame of mind, or state, in which another's emotions may be shared, held and understood (Craib, 2001, p.207), has verification in findings from neuroscience. Schore reports that a child fixates directly on a mother's eyes, the visible portion of the carer's central nervous system, which specifically reflect the activity and state of her right hemisphere; known to be dominant for gaze behaviour. This affords the child an opportunity to monitor the mother's internal states (Schore, 1994 p.75). The right hemisphere is also involved not just in the reception, but in the expression of affective states. Emotions are communicated to the face spontaneously and rapidly, stimulating motor responses in the observer's face. This describes an unconscious tendency to mimic and synchronize with another person's facial expression, gestures, movements and vocalizations (Schore, 2003, p.224). The discovery of mirror neurons in 1995 by Jeannerod, Arbib, Rizzolatti and Sakata (Cozolino 2002, p.186), suggest that phenomenon such as transference and counter-transference are constantly present in human communications and virtually impossible to avoid.

In Klein's paranoid-schizoid position, ambivalent feelings are split within the psyche (Hinshelwood, 1989, p. 156). Often the acceptable parts are retained by the self while the unacceptable are projected, or transferred onto another and experienced by the subject as if they are constructs of the object. The projection of unpalatable parts from subject to object may produce social phenomena such as the stereotype (Clarke, 2008, 114) or othering in the forms of racism or sexism, for example (Barnett, 2009, p.4).

While the depressive position in Klein's model seeks reparation once the split good-object and bad-object are apprehended as being one-whole again (Laplanche & Pontalis, 1973, p.114), another possible path for the subject is that of projective identification. Here, rather than seeking reparation, repressed and unacceptable elements which have split from conscious awareness are not just projected onto another, but into them; introjected by them. Projective identification occurs when another person is coerced into behaving in a manner framed and projected by the subject. Holmes and Bateman write, 'projective identification becomes a mutual process in which projector and recipient interact with one another at an unconscious level (Bateman & Holmes, 1995, p. 85).

The psycho-social approach is mindful of Klein's theory of unconscious defences against anxiety. Hollway and Jefferson speak of the defended subject; a position in which the interview subject may employ psychodynamic defence strategies in order to avoid confronting anxieties invoked by either the research topic or the act of being interviewed (Hollway & Jefferson, 2000, p 19). The converse position is also considered; that of the defended researcher. Attention to the researcher's responses and experience is only a part of the psycho-social methodology. Reflexivity can bring a deeper awareness of unconscious communication from the interview subject (Hollway & Jefferson, 2000, p 40), and sustained self reflection continues to bring new insights into view.

A psycho-social researcher takes an ethical stance towards the interview subject, considering duty of care to be of paramount importance (Clark, 2008, p.121). In addition, maintaining empathy and a sensitivity to the interview subject's experience includes using and ordering the subject's ordering and phrasing; to participate in a form of careful listening (Clark, 2008, p.121). In this sense, it is more a question of eliciting the subject's experience rather than seeking to penetrate their knowledge or put them to the question. The free association narrative in which the interview subject sometimes steers the course (Clark, 2008, p.121), may seem on the surface to lack focus but a wealth of experiential data can emerge, and it is this which reveals the gestalt of the interview subject.

Methodology adopted for the study:

For this study three approaches were chosen for gathering data for analysis:

      a). The social photo matrix method (Seivers, 2008).

      b) Free association interview.

      c) Reflexive review and analysis.

I identified the following steps that would need to be taken:

1) Identify and locate interview subjects; obtain permission to interview and arrange to meet with them.

2) Conduct the interviews and begin a continual process of reflexivity.

3) Conduct the social photo matrix with fellow psycho-social research colleagues.

4) Conduct sustained reflexive analysis.

On the surface: analysis of interview themes presented in the interviews.

Identifying and contacting a key representative from of each of the two faith groups is recounted in the reflexive journal. It also contains an account of how I came to conduct the interviews as a defended researcher.

A number of key themes presented themselves in each of the two interviews.

The church warden and his companion were aware that the Druids had no historical association with Avebury and did not acknowledge the validity of modern Paganism. 'Pagan really means, in my book, erm, people that don't believe in God'. This definition of Pagan is reminiscent of Hutton's *Pagan Religions of the Ancient British Isles*, which leans towards an anthropological and archaeological approach (Hutton, 1991, preface). In *Triumph of the Moon*, however, Hutton reinterprets Pagan as 'country folk' (Hutton, 1999, p. 4). It would appear that the church warden, who was also deputy curator for the Keiller Museum had read the archaeological book, but not the one leaning towards Witchcraft. There is a bookshop in Avebury which is stocked with the latest tittles in Paganism and Witchcraft. The implication here is that the church congregation may not understand the beliefs and practices which accompany some of those who come to village, and they avoid taking an action of discovery. I was told the locals treat the head Druid as a 'bit of a fun figure', and tolerance is the attitude of the church to the 'Pagans'. The church warden ended his interview by asserting, 'Well, I spoken too much; I was told I mustn't say too much, but ...'. which implies a gate-keeper had placed restrictions upon the interview.

The head Druid, the Keeper of the Stones, appeared relaxed during the interview. He told me in a jovial fashion that he regularly faced religious persecution from the villagers, though not specifically from the church. He became markedly animated when discussing the shortcomings and incompetence of other Druid leaders and was very scathing of Wiccans and Witches, calling them, '... Lazy Druids. The Wiccans have a set ritual ceremony, and that will answer all their problems; ritual ceremonies which is Catholicism; Catholicism in black ...'. His closing statement was that, 'I'm not a priest and it's not a religion. Mine's a belief system 'cos I

79

only work in arguable facts,' which possibly calls into question his presence on the Swindon College faith counsellors advice panel.

Other incongruences presented themselves, but the two themes that caught my attention during the interview was firstly the Christian refusal to acknowledge the validity of the Pagans as Pagans, rather than people not of God, and second being the Druid's rhetoric and dismissal of other Druid and Pagan groups. This appears to be a classic example of Freud's *Narcissism of Minor Differences* (Freud, 1921).

Additional themes presented themselves when I began my reflexive practice.

The Social Photo Matrix research method:

In *Organisational & Social Dynamics,* Seivers suggests, 'Perhaps it is the role of pictures to get in contact with the uncanny', using the social photo matrix as a method to promote the understanding of the unconscious in groups and organisations (Seivers, 2008). I decided to conduct this method of research with a small group, comprising three fellow students and a professor of psycho-social studies. The exercise with the group was also to include a free association response to two pages of transcript from my interview with the Druid. To avoid any bias in the technique, I elected to do the social photo matrix first.

After a brief presentation I showed the group five photographs of Avebury village and church, intending this to be a presentation of ordinary life in an English village, with no mention of the prehistoric temple. This was to be followed by five photographs of the Neolithic stones of Avebury, without showing any details of the village, intending this to be a presentation of an ordinary stone circle.

Finally, two photographs were presented showing Avebury in its complete form.

This was followed by the free association of the presented transcript.

Avebury in duality: village life:

Avebury in duality: Neolithic temple:

Avebury as a whole:

<u>The social photo matrix and free association prompted responses which
yielded unexpected data:</u>

The first student to speak said that I appear to be passionate about the
place, and second asserted that I seem to hold a romantic view towards
the stones. One concluded that I had more sympathy with the Druids,
although that particular student may have been unconsciously referring
to his own position, 'Makes you want to get down with the Druids rather
than the Christians.'

The professor of psycho-social studies pointed out that there were no
people in any of the photographs. The group looked puzzled as the
realisation dawned and it was noted that in the temple pictures there was
no modernity, while the village pictures had normal ordinary life;
exemplified in one showing a romantic thatched cottage with a car parked
outside. A student remarked that he felt 'at home' when looking at the
village pictures, but the stones 'left him cold; the village represented the
familiarity of rural England while the stones could be anywhere'. The
discussion moved to the signpost that has the word, 'World' at its centre,
perhaps suggesting that Avebury is a place where ancient and modern,
secular and faith converge.

It was suggested that I could have made the church area more beautiful in
the photographs; I acknowledge they are not as aesthetic as the stones. It
was noted: there is a 'beautiful thatched cottage', and 'small villages are
about people, about community'. It was pointed out that 'this is a social
study with no people in it'. I replied that I wanted to see if the
photographs would convey the differences of community without the
images of people; is the landscape by itself indicative of the society it
holds ?

A turn in orientation: an emergent theme and a new identity for the study

The morning after the social photo matrix and free association, I awoke in a state of reflexive awareness. I realised that my research focus was not the interrelational dynamics of the two main faith groups of Avebury; it was their relationship to the landscape. After more reflection an understanding emerged that what I am interested in is the relationship between landscape and identity. When reviewing my decisions, I became aware of how my unconscious had steered me along this path all along. For example:

- I had unconsciously decided to take photos of place with no people

- I asked questions in the interviews which addressed issues of territory, ownership and invasion.

My choice of study was to look at two faith groups who each tolerate the 'other' in their sacred space, and yet neither group has legitimate claim to the origins of the Avebury temple. Further reflexivity brought an awareness of more material than this paper can accommodate. There were, however, three key themes, and it is these I shall address.

- Group dynamics.

- Landscape and ritual practice as a secure base.

- Landscape and identity: a relational perspective.

Beneath the surface: analysis of interview themes which emerged from sustained reflexive practice.

Group dynamics

In attachment, evolution and the psychology of religion, Kirkpatrick postulates that Christians, and possibly followers of other monotheist religions, may form attachment style relationships with God; in effect, God becomes a secure base. Contrasting this, the deity groups of polytheistic religions have features which are less like attachment dynamics and more akin to social relationships; each deity has a specialised role and the worshiper forms a unique relationship with both the role and the deity (Kirkpatrick,2005, p.92). With regard to religious or spiritual leaders, Kirkpatrick stresses that attachments are formed with the person and not the role. Various people may play the role of temporary caregiver in a child's life, but attachment bonds are formed with specific individuals. Likewise, it is possible that a particular vicar or Druid priest may form attachment relationships with individuals who are followers, and strong bonds may be forged, but these do not necessarily constitute an attachment relationship with the role itself. On the surface, it may be tempting to form a superficial opinion that the Gods and Goddesses of the Druids and Pagans of Avebury are merely figures of mythical fantasy who only serve to constitute a set of projected objects; the pantheon taking the form of a network of social relations. However, the power of the affect released and expressed in relation to Avebury and other megalithic temples in Britain suggests that these places which feature enduringly in the landscape evoke powerful affectionate bonds. Visitors to ancient places can sometimes become aware of a sense of being a temporary performer on a permanent stage (Pearson, 2003). The continuity of the sacred monument within the landscape creates the conditions in which Avebury may become a secure base for followers of pluralist belief systems.

Landscape and ritual practice as a secure base

The historical continuity of the Avebury landscape provides a secure base for both the Christians and Pagans who reside there. Religious practice also has an enduring quality which allows patterns of social attachment and altruism to emerge (Kirkpatrick, 2005, p.257) and become neuro-associated (Bandler & Grinder, 1979, p.83) with both the community and its container environment. In addition, the landscape appears to represent a secure base for those who regularly attend the site while following a pattern of reverence and ritual. Berry, an author of a series of fictional works based in Pagan society testifies, 'I personally find security and grounding in the framework of the Wheel of the Year with its symbols and focus on movement and change' (Berry, 2009). It would seem that contemporary Pagan culture functions as an autopoietic system, gaining its structure from an attachment to both ritual that is located within time and to place (Capra, 1996, p.213).

For the Druids, Pagans and Christians of Avebury, whether resident or regular visitor, the landscape carved by Neolithic, Bronze age and Iron age hands represents a home for their spiritual practice; a place where matters of faith can reside. In *Geographies of Exclusion*, Sibley describes the fabric of the home as, 'a place where space and objects together provide aesthetic experiences and evoke memories' (Sibley, 1995, p.94).

Landscape and identity: a relational perspective.

The projection of identity into the landscape and the appropriation of the landscape's identity is evident with both the Druidic and Christian cultures of Avebury. During my interview with the Keeper of the Stones, the young people gathered were told that the curve on the south western embankment had been shaped deliberately by the Henge builders in order to specifically allow the setting of the Sun on the spring equinox to be observable for a slightly longer period of time; the gentle sloping of the bank did appear to hold the disc of the sun deliberately. However, it is easy for a modern mind to mistakenly interpret archaeological sites though a contemporary lens and for the external landscape to become imbued with a cultural mythos that is sometimes based on error, misunderstandings or on simply being uninformed. Five thousand years of English weather beating against the once high embankment of Avebury has taken its toll on both its height and shape (Wheatley & Taylor, 2008, p.6). An uninformed person viewing the passage of the Solar disc brushing the top of the south western embankment may mistakenly assume that it was designed that way. The suggestion by the Keeper of the Stones that, 'they did it this way because ...', reveals not only that he asserts power by suggesting he is the keeper of exclusive knowledge; 'We create a wall of superstition about what we did to sustain our magic', (Sibley,1995, p.120),. There is also a tacit relational attachment of the contemporary Druid order to the Neolithic builders of Avebury.

In *Geographies of Exclusion*, Sibley asserts that the ambivalence attached to stereotyped others may also be attached to place; a simultaneous repulsion and desire (Sibley, 1995, p.100). It may be tempting to presume that the Christian community of Avebury is indifferent, dismissive, disdainful or fearful towards the Pagan stones that surround their village; the church warden does tell us these were placed here by, in his definition, a Godless people. It was with some surprise that I learned that two stones recently excavated on the far western edge of the site have been named by the villagers. I suggest this shows that landscape and identity are both introjective and intrajective. Two sets of relational nicknames have given to the pair of stones; the first pair-name mentioned has its roots in British cultural folk law; Jack and Jill. On the surface, this appears to be indicative of a familiarisation, suggesting the formation of an affectionate bond with the new object in the landscape. The second set of nicknames suggest there is also something deeper beneath the surface; Adam and Eve. The two objects which originate from a Godless society of innocents, worshiped in the present day by, false Pagans who have turned from God, have now become identified with not only the first two names in the bible, but the first two names of anyone to walk the earth. This suggests a deep rooted appropriation of identity; a need for inclusion that brings the two external stones within the sanctuary of Christianlty.

The landscape of Avebury may be viewed as a blank canvas for the imagination to play with. Its Neolithic shapes are alien to modern iconography and those within its landscape are somehow encouraged to participate in the search for meaning and identity; to find a secure base in a changing world that flows through an enduring place of history. I was told of a woman who would regularly travel across the county of Wiltshire to Avebury by taxi and insist that the church warden accompany her around the site while she, 'points out the faces she could see in the stones' (sic). The church warden also spoke of the many visitors who believe Avebury to be a spaceship, and not merely a relic of one from a long past visitation. Some believe that it is an alien landing site and that on some occasion in the future, superior beings from an order of a higher intelligence will return, suggesting that the believer's identification with having a higher intelligence has split from conscious identity and is projected on to something higher than the self, upwards into the stars. However, as delusionary as these beliefs may seem to an outsider, it has been shown there is a correlation between Neolithic sites, the landscape and the cosmos. Clive Ruggles, Britain's first professor of archeoastronomy writes;

> In recent years, archaeologists have become increasingly aware that patterns of human activity within the prehistoric landscape are likely to have been influenced by more than just ecological and economic factors. Ancient landscapes might also have been structured according to symbolic or cosmological principles, forming what have become known as 'sacred geographies'. Specific places, and indeed whole landscapes, are 'contexts for human

experience, constructed in movement, memory, encounter and association'. (Ruggles, 1999, p.120).

The prehistoric landscape of Avebury; rich in symbolism and aesthetically shaped by its crafted horizon to be a container for a ritualistic community, appears to retain its power to inspire affective relational dynamics with the faith groups and worshipers who find an enduring security within its landscape.

Conclusion:

I have shown in this study that the relationship between landscape and identity may be both introjective and intrajective; each impressing itself upon the other.

Avebury, a Neolithic landscape encompassing both a Pagan temple and English village, acts as a container, holding and possibly regulating the affect of the faith groups within its boundaries. It would appear that Avebury comes to represent a secure base for the faith groups that reside within its symbolic landscape because of the continuity in which they are held. This, I suggest, fosters a tolerance which serves to underpin the peaceful stability of the Christian-Pagan community. I have placed the hyphen between the two faith groups of the community with deliberate care. I suggest that an autopoiesis is also at play here; there is a structural coupling between the two communities who are beginning to acknowledge and give value to one another. The continuity of both place and timed ritual, in addition to the affect regulation fostered by the attachment to a secure base of containment, appear to be significant factors in the embryonic, emergent reparation between the faith groups of Avebury.

The reflexive material produced from the attending to the progressive emergence of the researcher's counter-transference can add an enriched dynamic to the research that may not have been available had this methodology not been undertaken. The psycho-social approach in using subjectivity as a research instrument brings to light that which is beneath the surface.

Bibliography:

Avebury Tourist Information Centre,
http://www.ukinformationcentre.com/southern-england/avebury-tourist-information-centre.htm, sourced 18th February, 2009.

Bandler, R. and Grinder, J., 1979, *Frogs into Princes*, Real People Press.

Bandler, R, and Grinder, J, 1975, *The Structure of Magic 1*, Science and Behavior books.

Barnett, C , p.4, *Ways of Relating: Hospitality and the Acknowledgement of Otherness*,
http://oro.open.ac.uk/7142/1/Ways_of_Relating_PHG_Final.pdf, sourced, 27th April 2009.

Bateman, Anthony and Holmes, Jeremy, 1995, *Introduction to Psychoanalysis*, Routledge.

BBC, *Thousands mark summer solstice*,

http://news.bbc.co.uk/1/hi/england/wiltshire/7465235.stm, sourced, 4th May 2009.

Berry, K, *personal communication from the author*; email received 30th April 2009.

Capra, F, 1996, The Web of Life, Harper Collins.

Clarke, S., 2008, *Object Relations and Social Relations*, Karnac Books.

Cozolino, L, 2002, The Neuroscience of Psychotherapy, W. W. Norton and Company

Craib, I., 2001, *Psychoanalysis, a critical introduction*, Polity Press.

English Heritage,
http://www.wessexarch.co.uk/files/Learning/avebury_teachers_kit/history_of_the_avebury_monuments.pdf, sourced 26th April 2009.

Freud, S., 1921, *Group Psychology and the Analysis of the Ego, S.E.,* 18:65-143 (Chapter 6).

Freud, S.,1931, *The Disposition to Obsessional Neurosis,* G.W. , VIII, 445; S.E., XII, 320. Cited in: Laplanche & Pontalis, *The Language of Psychoanalysis,* 1973, W.W. Norton and Company.

Fryer, J., *Druid wars: how a drunken row over 4000 year old bones in causing chaos in pagan circles,* http://www.dailymail.co.uk/news/article-1127430/Druid-wars-How-drunken-row-4-000-year-old-bones-causing-chaos-pagan-circles.html, sourced 18th February 2009.

Harrison, M., 2001, *The Master Practitioner Suite Volumes One, Two and Three,* Tao Te Publishing.

Hawkes Steve, *Revisiting Britain's biggest free festival,*

http://news.bbc.co.uk/1/hi/entertainment/music/3662921.stm, sourced 26th April 2009.

Hinshelwood, R. D., 1989, *A dictionary of Kleinian thought,* Free Association Press.

Hoggett, P., 2008, *Object Relations and Social Relations,* Karnac Books.

Holloway, W. Jefferson, T., 2000, *Doing Qualitive Research Differently,* Sage.
Holloway, W., 2008, *Object Relations and Social Relations,* Karnac Books.

Hutton, R., 1991, *The Pagan Religions of the Ancient British Isles,* Basil Blackwell Ltd.

Hutton, R., 1999, *The Triumph of the Moon,* Oxford University Press.

Hutton, R., 2007, *The Druids,* Hambledon Continuum.

Kirkpatrick, L. A., 2005, *Attachment, Evolution and the Psychology of Religion,* The Guildford Press.

Lackey, J, Sosa, E., 2006, *The Epistemology of Testimony*, Oxford University Press.

Laplanche & Pontalis, 1973, *The Language of Psychoanalysis*, W.W. Norton and Company.

Mudhar, R., *Stonehenge*, http://www.anlma.demon.co.uk/stonehenge/index.html, sourced 30th April 2009.

Ogden, T.H., 1999, Reverie and Interpretation, Karnac Books.

Orbach, S., 2008, *Object Relations and Social Rleations*, Karnac Books.

Panayi May, *Avebury Stone Circle and Silbury Hill*, http://www.history.uk.com/articles/index.php?archive=57, sourced, 26th April 2009

Pearson, B., 2003, *filled with awe (Stonehenge)*, http://www.dooyoo.co.uk/destinations-national/stonehenge/425772/, sourced 4th May 2009.

Ruggles, C., 1999, *Astronomy in Prehistoric Britain and Ireland*, Yale University Press.

Schore, A., 1994, *Affect Regulation and Origin of the Self*, Lawrence Erlbaum Associates Inc.

Schore, A., 2003, *Affect Regulation and the Repair of the Self*, W. W. Norton and Company.

Seivers, B., 2008, *Organisational & Social Dynamics,* 8, 2: 234-254

Sibley, D., 1995, *Geographies of Exclusion*, Routeledge.

Swindon College multi faith team, http://www.swindon-college.ac.uk/index.php?option=com_content&task=view&id=46, sourced 18th February 2009.

Wheatley, M, Taylor, B, 2009, *Avebury: Sun, Moon and Earth*, Wessex.

Wilkinson M, 2006, *Coming into Mind*, Routledge.

Wiltshire Council,
http://www.wiltshire.gov.uk/community/getchurch.php?id=11, sourced
26th April 2009.

What roles may discourse, narrative and literalism play in the making and resolution of conflict?

The kernel of this paper is to consider the phenomenological relationship between experience, language and behaviour. The initial step toward answering the question of this paper will be an explanation of the literal; the neuroscience of experience and the constructs of the emergence of consciousness and language. The making of meaning and belief is explored, before considering the relationship between discourse and behaviour. Literalism is viewed from two perspectives: the autistic spectrum and its role in the constructs of religious fundamentalism. The paper will show how language and belief relate to the emotional systems of an individual and their role in the regulation of affect.

The Narrative Self:

Stephen Pinker attests that humans have an instinct for language; 'Language is so tightly woven into human experience it is scarcely possible to imagine life without it' (Pinker, 1994, p.17). Words are not merely symbolic conveyers of ideas or meaning; the phenomena of language is a construct of what may be considered to be that which defines being human; a complex and sophisticated consciousness of self (Dennet, 1991, p.191). Consciousness does not appear to arise from any single region or neural network of the brain, but appears to be an emergent function which arises from the integration and synchrony of cycles of neural processing (Cozolino, 2002, p153). In *The Feeling of What Happens*, Domasio describes the emergence of narrative as a process which begins with a proto-conscious core self:

> ...neural patterns which become images, images being the same fundamental currency in which the description of the consciousness-causing object is also carried out. Most importantly, the images that constitute this narrative are incorporated in the stream of thoughts. The images in the con-sciousness narrative flow like shadows along with the images of the object for which they are providing an unwitting, unsolicited comment. To come back to the metaphor of movie-in-the-brain, they are *within* the movie. There is no external spectator (Domasio, 1999, p171).

Domasio asserts the autobiographical self is constituted by implicit memories of multiple instances of past experiences which grow continuously and may be partly remodelled to reflect new experiences. Sets of memories which describe identity and person can be reactivated as a neural pattern and made explicit as images (Domasio, 1999, p.174). Edelman and Tononi confer, describing the formation of the autobiographical self as, 'the remembered present', a higher-order of consciousness which can place itself in a scheme of the past, present and anticipated future, which, in its most developed form has a semantic and linguistic capability (Edelman and Tononi, 2000, p. 103).

Language and the Making of Meaning: Constructs of Conceptual Reality

In *Language, Consciousness and Culture*, Ray Jackendoff writes, 'The term of art for the form in which consciousness presents itself is qualia'. (Jackendoff, 2007, p.79). Qualia refers to a specific qualities of experience, such as: loudness, warmth and colour. Qualia are derived from a primary sensation, corresponding to unique states in the dynamic core. Tononi and Edelman report that these states are, '...differentiated from billions of other states within a neural space comprising a large number of dimensions. The relevant dimensions are given by the number of neuronal groups whose activities, integrated through reentrant interactions, constitute a dynamic core of high complexity. Qualia are therefore high-dimensional discriminations' (Edelman and Tononi, p. 175).

The topography of language may be viewed as a phonological, syntactic and semantic or conceptual in structure (Jackendoff, 2007, p.81). In *The Neuroscience of Psychotherapy*, Cozolino describes the networks of the semantic aspects of language explicitly:

> Although the semantic aspects of language are usually lateralized to the left hemisphere, the right contributes the emotional and prosodic element of speech. The left-hemisphere language network relies on the convergence of auditory, visual, and sensory information from the temporal, occipital, and parietal lobes, respectively. Wernicke's area in the temporal lobe receives input from the primary auditory area, and organizes it into meaningful bits of information. The convergence zone connects sounds, sights, and touch so that cross-modal connections can be made, allowing us to name things we touch and hear without visual cues.

These sophisticated networks are also called into play when a memory is recalled;

> It is also necessary for the development of sign language, where words take the form of gestures.

This sophisticated and highly processed information projects forward to Broca's area, where expressive speech is organized. Nerve fibers linking language areas to the rest of the frontal lobes allow both spoken and internal language to guide behavior and regulate affect. The integrative properties of language may be unequaled by any other function of the brain. Creating and recalling a story requires the convergence of multisensory emotional, temporal, and memory capabilities that bridge all vectors of neural networks. In this way, language organizes the brain and can be used to reorganize it in psychotherapy .

Qualia are discriminated through an experiential filter that reflects an individual's history of being (Edelman and Tononi, p. 175), while meaning and belief play interlocking and complementary roles in the interpretation of speech; this relationship is strengthened by emphasizing the connection between our grounds for attributing beliefs to speakers, and our grounds for assigning meanings to their utterances (Davidson, 1974, cited in Martinich, 2001, p.464).

Every human being has a set of experiences which constitute a unique personal history. This paper has shown the conceptual models of reality that we create in the process of living are based upon our individual experiences, and, since some aspects of our experiences will be unique, some parts of our model of the world will be singular to each of us (Bandler and Grinder, 1975, p. 12).

The Relational Self and Affect Regulation: an Attachment System Perspective

John Bowlby postulated a universal human need to form close affectional bonds (Bowlby, 1979, p. 82). Attachment theory describes a process by which a vulnerable human being seeks close proximity to a secure base whenever a threat is perceived. What might be termed 'attachment behaviours'; such as touching, soothing and holding, serve to strengthen the bond between the person whose anxiety system has been triggered and the person, most usually a primary care giver, who represents a secure base. The activation of attachment behaviours is dependant upon the evaluation of a threat and the goal of the attachment system is to regulate emotion and bring about a return to a feeling of security (Fonagay et al, 2002, p. 36).

In *Affect Regulation and the Repair of the Self*, Alan Schore reports, '… regulation theory suggests that attachment is, in essence, the right brain regulation of biological synchronicity between organisms' (Schore, 2003, p. 41). He continues;

> The right hemisphere contributes to the development of reciprocal interactions within the mother-infant regulatory system and mediates the capacity for biological synchronicity, the regulatory mechanism of attachment. Due to its role in regulating biological synchronicity between organisms, the activity of this hemisphere is instrumental to the empathic perception of the emotional states of other human beings. The interactive regulation of right brain attachment biology is thus the substrate of empathy (Schore, 2003, p. 44).

Complexity and Social Relations:

Dynamic Systems Theory illuminates new areas of understanding in the field of social psychology. Concepts such as Structural Coupling and Autopoiesis describe the interrelationality of individuals and how groups or complex systems of groups are self-maintaining and self regulating, allowing for changes within their internal systems which contribute to their successful maintenance (Capra, 1996, p. 213). Other theories such as Interpersonal Synchronization describe how groups of people become attuned to one another over long periods of time in which individuals are not passive entities but instead are separate systems capable of displaying rich dynamics, with each individual adjusting its internal state in response to the state or behaviour of the person with whom they are reacting. Negating correlations can occur in certain contexts, such as the silence of a listener while a speaker is talking, or in the satisfaction or happiness of one individual as another feels sadness or despair (Guastello et al, 2009, p. 388).

Reflexive Note:

I think it appropriate during the course of this paper to offer a reflexive note from my own perceptual perspective. I am an adult with Asperger's Syndrome and as such I have often experienced social exclusion; both emotionally and linguistically. Writing a paper for a module entitled Conflict, Communication and Transformation constitutes something of a paradox for me because I tend to spend much of my life actively seeking to avoid conflict. While this means I do not have many personal experiences of conflict I can draw upon, viewing life through the lens of the autistic spectrum does provide me with a non-typical insight into a specific realm of human social interaction with which conflict may be resolved; communication.

Literalism; An Asperger's Syndrome Perspective:

Since Kaner and Asperger listed the phenomena and symptoms of autism syndromes psychologists from a wide variety of fields have sought to fully understand the autistic spectrum (Sacks, 1995, p. 234). While there are a wide range of variations, one of the common themes among those with high-functioning autism, or Asperger's Syndrome, is a tendency towards literalism.

Paxton and Estay report, 'One of the hallmarks of the autistic spectrum is their propensity to think visually', (Paxton and Estay, 2007, p. 50). Not only would I agree with this statement, but I found upon first reading their attempt to describe what they think an Asperger's thinking experience to be like, uncannily accurate;

> People on the autism spectrum are often literal thinkers (Happe 1995; Martin and McDonald 2004; Noens and van Berckelaer-Onnes 2004; Ogletree and Fischer 1995). Figures of speech confuse them, and are misunderstood. It is this writer's guess that this colloquialism confusion makes sense from a visual thinking perspective, as many figures of speech do not make sense as pictures. Take the example of the expression of raining cats and dogs. What would it look like to have cats and dogs falling from the sky? What would it sound like? What image comes to mind when thinking about cats and dogs hitting the ground from that height? The visual image is rather gruesome, don't you think? Feeling blue ? How does that make sense? Does that mean you would have blue skin? The thought of having a frog in your throat might be rather disturbing. If someone called you a smart Alec, would that mean you were dumb if your name was Bill? It does not take many colloquialisms to demonstrate that they would be confusing to someone who is a visual and literal thinker.

Literal thinking can also mean that there is no underlying meaning. Words are taken at face value and hidden meanings are left unexplored. I tend to speak in long-hand, doing my best to complete all sentences and ensure that I clarify any unspecified pronouns. Literalism may also mean being very specific in thought and communication. I often experience my verbal speech as a visual text that is being written just out in front of my vision, and I attempt to make it as tidy and linear as possible, in real time. Unfortunately, this is also how I hear people and fractured sentences, unspecified pronouns, jumbled tenses and unfamiliar figures of speech cause a great deal of confusion. In my Asperger's world, confusion is experienced as a form of physical pain; it is always accompanied by a high level of anxious vulnerability and a desire to return to a secure base of safety.

Literalism in Religious Fundamentalism

In *the Psychology of Religious Fundamentalism*, Wood et al, present a model for understanding the thought process of fundamentalism without reference to any specific dogma or religion; although their work remains primarily with the three Abrahamic religions; Judaism, Christianity and Islam. The model is described as Intratextual, since it makes no reference to the religious content; only the psychological process. The model is comprised of three elements; Sacred Texts, Absolute Truths and the Principle of Intratextuality. The first principle focuses on the reading of a sacred text which will speak in its own way to the reader. The second, the acceptance that this text is sacred and thirdly, it is an absolute truth (Wood et al, 2005, p. 22).

Hoggett, in *Politics, Identity and Emotion*, describes fundamentalist behaviours in psychoanalytic terms, suggesting that both Christian and Islamic fundamentalism are reactions to the threat of modernity; as if a collective form of paranoid-schizoid psychosis is at play (Hoggett, 2009, p. 96). While I would not dispute these findings, I would like to present another hypothesis.

<u>Narratives of Exclusion: Exploring the Theological Roots of the Abrahamic
Religions and the Discourse of 'Othering':</u>

Kirkpatrick suggests that for some people, a theology, religion or even
God may represent a secure base (Kirkpatrick, 2005, p. 65). This
hypothesis brings clarity to Hoggett's observations regarding the
psychosis of fundamentalist behaviour, in which the fundamentalists
display what Hoggett refers to as concrete thinking in their literalism
towards their sacred text (Hoggett, 2009, p. 103). I would like to propose,
the fundamentalist reaction towards modernity may also be understood
as a desire to regain a closer proximity with the heart of their religious
theology.

Zoroastrianism was the major belief system in the Middle East before
Islam. Its texts share common roots with Sanskrit and it is estimated to
have originated between 588 and 1900 BCE (Watson, 2005, p. 112).
Zoroastrianism has elements of the cult of Mithras, Hinduism, Buddhism
and Confucianism and helped form some of the core principles of
Judaism, Christianity and Islam. Chief among these was a view of the
afterlife; a House of Song which contained a bridge dividing the just and
the wicked. Ideas of judgment, Heaven and Hell, and of a great battle
between forces of good and evil were Zoroastrian in origin. The three
Abrahamic religions are the only religions, as far as the author is aware,
that give a specific name to people outside of its own group. If you are not
a Jew, you are a Gentile. If you are not a Christian you are a Heretic, and if
you are not a Muslim you are an Infidel. To suggest that a linguistic habit
of 'othering' is ubiquitous among the texts and subtle unconscious daily
language of not just followers of the Abrahamic religions, but those who
reside within the coverage of its medias, at this stage in the research may
appear to be little more than conjecture. However, from the perspective
of an individual who is immersed in the media streams of popular culture,
it would seem that the precepts of 'us and them' have woven themselves
into the cloth of cultural discourse; the scripts and plot lines of soap
operas, films, poems and pop songs feature battles between light and
dark and it is 'them', or 'they', who are wrong, at fault or evil. Further
research would be required to investigate the possibility of whether,
through the subtle discourses of othering, collective synchronized
relational systems, or groups, of population are affectively primed for
conflict via the media in its various forms.

A Discursive Approach to Social Change

Fairclough describes the process of discursive change and how it leads to changes in social convention, combining aspects of a Foucoultian view with a Bakhtinian emphasis on intertextuality. (Fairclough, 1992, p. 96). He reports, 'Change involves forms of transgression, crossing boundaries, such as putting together existing conventions in new combinations, or drawing upon conventions which usually preclude them' (Fairclough, 1992, p. 96).

Change may also leave traces in texts in the form of co-occurrence of contradictory or inconsistent elements, comprising formal and informal styles, technical and informal vocabularies and markers of authority or familiarity. Discursive change emerges and solidifies into a transformed convention; contradictory texts soon begin to blend, their boundaries becoming seamless. This naturalising process is essential for establishing new hegemonies in discourse. Fairclough also reports that rearticulating discourses into new hegemonies may bring about localised changes in discourse which may culminate and transcend institutions and affect the societal order of discourse (Fairclough, 1992, p. 97).

Non-Violent Communication

Lederach asserts, 'Conflict transformation is an approach which recognizes conflict is a normal and continuous dynamic within human relationships' (Lederarch, 2003, p. 15). The ability to take an alternative view, to re-position or re-frame the meaning of an event by adjusting the narrative with which we describe it, is an effective strategy for initiating relational change (Grinder & Bandler, 1981, p. 137). Among many other possible models for resolving conflict, which the constraints of space in this paper preclude the writer of this paper from exploring, Deutsch et al outline an approach of non-violent communication. Initially, empathy rather than statements of evaluation are employed in a manner which maintains the status values of all parties concerned. The second stage is that of appreciative enquiry, with a view to foster faith and cooperation alongside a mutual desire for change. Powerful non-defensive communication is advocated, suggesting communication be constructive and compassionate; relating is reciprocal and respectful. Constructive communication, it is suggested, bears the hallmarks of cordial caring language and a sense of self awareness for one's own manipulative messages (Deutsch et al, 2006, p. 171).

Two Examples of Transforming Personal Conflicts and Community
Tensions using Narrative and Discursive Approaches

Holding the other person's value as a constant is a vital element in the Neuro Linguistic Programming (NLP) approach towards enabling individuals to change and transform their lives. Practitioners guide their clients towards achieving states of self empowerment within a wide variety of contexts; from resolving drug addictions to Olympic coaching. In most cases, the problem has its roots in a dilemma or paradox; one part of the individual's personality wants one thing while another part has a different agenda in mind. Initiating a dialogue between the two parts begins a transition which, if successful, transforms the conflict into the desired outcome.

The same process can be utilised to ease community tensions. In the city of Bristol, Hen Wilkinson has set up a community conflict support group called Community Resolve. Their work, performed on behalf of local communities, serves as an exemplary model of conflict transformation in practice. The most easily observable example, the conscious element of Community Resolve, may be found in work such as encouraging youth workers to interact and talk to community police officers. In a small and neutral environment, each party is   encouraged to exchange ideas and experiences; before long, dialogues are interwoven and meanings interchanged. The symbiotic relationship between youth worker and community policeman has begun.

However, much of Community Resolve's work is more subtle and perhaps unseen; generating discussions with community groups at which concepts of conflict are 're-framed' into new paradigms. By viewing conflict as a necessary stage of growth and transformation, or the debate of conflict viewed in the light of democracy in action, Hen Wilkinson can be seen to be pioneering the application of generating new discursive pathways which will regulate affects among communities and propagate peace.

Conclusion

This paper shows the relationships between experience, language and behaviour. The emergence of conscious awareness as a narrative of the autobiographical self is explored in relation to external linguistic influences. The paper describes the role of discourse in social change and how literalism can generate narrow ranges of choice in behaviour and give rise to extremism. Language is shown to play a key role at the heart of belief and theology and may be employed in the making or resolution of conflict. The subtle distinction between conflict resolution and transformation has been discussed prior to examples being shown of both an individual and collective instance of these theories in practice.

The themes presented in this paper represent a broad range of topics and fields of study. At the time of writing, the depth of research in each topic varies considerably, especially among emergent disciplines. While the space given to this paper places a constraint upon the depth to which each has been explored, it has given an opportunity for the author to introduce themes for future research and study.

Bibliography:

Bandler, R., Grinder J., 1975, *The Structure of Magic*, Science and Behaviour Books.

Bowlby, J., 1979, The Making and Breaking of Affectional Bonds, Tavistock Publications

Capra, F., 1996, *The Web of Life*, HarperCollins.

Cozolino, L., 2002, *The Neuroscience of Psychotherapy*, W.W. Norton and Company inc.

Davidson, D., 1974, *Belief and the Basis of Meaning*, cited in Martininch, A. P., *ed*, (2001), *The Philosophy of Language*. Oxford: Oxford university Press.

Deutsch, M., Coleman, P., Marcus, E, 2006, *The Handbook of Conflict Resolution*, John Wiley & Sons, Inc.

Domasio, A., 1999, *The Feeling of What Happens*, William Heinemann.

Edelman, G M, Tononi, G., 2000, *Consciousness: How Matter Becomes Imagination*, Allen Lane The Penguin Press.

Fonagay, P, Gergely, G, Elliot J, Target M, 2004, *Affect Regulation, Mentalization, and the Development of the Self*, ITC Bookman.

Fairclough N, 1994, *Discourse and Social Change*, Polity Press.

Grinder, J., Bandler, R., 1981, Trance-formations, Real People Press.

Guastello S, Koopmans M, Pincus D, 2009, Chaos and Complexity in Psychology, Cambridge University Press.

Hoggett. P., 2009, *Politics, Identity and Emotion*, Paradigm, Boulder, Colorado.

Hood, R W, Jr, Hill Peter C, Williamson W Paul, 2005, *The Psychology of Religious Fundamentalism*, The Guildford Press.

Jackendorff R, 2007, Language, Consciousness, Culture; Essays on Mental Structure, The MIT Press.

Kirkpatrick L A, 2005, *Attachment, Evolution, And The Psychology of Religion*, The Guildford Press.

Davidson D, *Belief and the Basis of Meaning* – in Martinich A. P., *The Philosophy of Language*, 2001, The Oxford University Press.

Lederach J P, 2003, *The Little Book Of Conflict Transformation*, Good Books.

Paxton K, Estay I A, 2007, *Counselling People on the Autism Spectrum*, Jessica Kingsley Publishers.

Pinker S, 1994, *the Language Instinct*, Penguin Books.

Sacks O, 1995, An Anthropologist on Mars, Picador.

Schore A N, 2003, Affect Regulation And The Repair Of the Self, W.W. Norton & Company, Inc.

Watson P, Ideas: 2005, A History from Fire To Freud, Weidenfield & Nicolson.

Determinism and Agency in Affective Neuroscience:

a Psycho-Social perspective

Being a Dissertation Submitted in part requirement for the degree of MSc Psycho-Social Studies at the University of the West of England (Bristol) Faculty of Humanities, Languages and Social Sciences.

Dissertation Supervisor: Nigel Williams
Date: 4th May 2010

Abstract:

Historically, the nature versus nurture debate has divided approaches in psychology. However, recent advances in technology have further illuminated the relationship between the brain and behaviour, while interdisciplinary concepts of non-linear dynamical systems have brought new insights to understanding the embodied psychology of human nature. This study will review both determinism and agency primarily in affective neuroscience and will be supported by findings in the theories of both complexity and epigentics. The investigation of determinism and agency will be undertaken with two approaches. Initially it will review the literature of determinism in the fields of genetics, affective neuroscience and complexity theory. The role of the environment in determinism will be considered before undertaking a summary review of neuroplasticity in the mature adult brain. The final parts of the study will review the transformational process of the therapeutic relationship in talking therapies such as psychotherapy, neuro linguistic programming and hypnotherapy, as a way of addressing the role of the environment in relation to determinism, agency and volition. The affective neuroscience of agency and volition will be surveyed before an appraisal of the study, which will include references to a small scale sample of psycho-social research, previously undertaken in preliminary modules.

Table of contents: Page No.

Title and Abstract: 127

Introduction: 131

Affective Neuroscience: 135

Determinism: an innate predisposition of nature: 137

The role of the environment in determinism: 143

The nurturing of nature: the predisposition of a relational self: 145

Adult brain development and neural plasticity: 157

Finding new pathways in the therapeutic environment: 161

Agency: the sense of self and the free will of volition in
affective neuroscience: 167

Reflections on the study: a review of how the findings of
the study relate to previous psycho-social research: 177

Recapitulation: 179

Reflexive note: 185

Conclusion: 189

Bibliography: 190

Introduction:

In my astrological practice I am frequently asked questions regarding fate and free-will. My reply is often met with surprise; contrary to expectation, I do not advocate any typological approach to understanding human nature and neither am I a fatalist. To date, my position regarding determinism has been an intuitive understanding that we have an innate nature which is then nurtured. The question of whether we are directed by a fated causality or whether we are beings with complete freedom of will has been a focus of attention in the philosophy of ancient cultures, and particularly that of the Greeks (Dennet, 1984, p. 1). The Stoic position was that existence is fated and that one must resign to it by adjusting one's expectations downwards to meet circumstances. This was known as 'apatheia', and is the etymological root of its contemporary reductive 'apathy' (Dennet, 1984, p. 2). Conversely, Plato advocated a belief that fate is negotiable. The Greek's framework of fate is that the universe came into existence as a compound of reason; which is the attribute of God, and that of necessity; which is the attribute of physical existence. To give in to physical passion is to be subject to necessity. To control such passion helps the individual return to reason (Campion, 2008, P. 165). The Aristotelian perspective was that the universe had agency or 'will', and that the soul is a means of both cognition and movement. In turn, this is subject to movements of the planets in the celestial sphere, which are however, secondary causes, transmitting the will of the prime-mover. This perspective held sovereignty in the philosophy of the understanding of fate until Plato's belief reemerged as Neo-Platonism in the Renaissance (Tester, 1987, p. 205). A popular belief in fate was superseded by a Cartesian mechanism; the scientific model of the world-machine (Capra, 1996, p. 19). It was not until 1905 that a new voice pronouncing on the nature of fate arose in a philosophical landscape which now featured Darwin's natural selection and the transformational science of psychoanalytic psychotherapy. Alan Leo, an English astrologer, stated, 'Character is Destiny' (Curry, 1992, p. 159). In the light of this declaration, the question now arises; what creates character and can fate be negotiated by a re-negotiation of character?

The debate of nature and nurture, or fate and freewill, has a broader implication than being just a matter of philosophy; it is a debate that reaches into the heart of the question of personal responsibility and culpability for one's actions. Pinker reports that, 'Cognitive scientists are sometimes approached by criminal defence lawyers in the hope that a wayward pixel on a brain scan might exonerate their client.' (Pinker, 2002, p. 176). He suggests that understanding the biology and neurology of human behaviour prompts a fearful reaction among people who assume that if our biology or the brain plays a role in determining our identity or character, then personal responsibility is in some way diminished by having a scientific explanation of behaviour, like a bio-causality. In other words, 'my brain made me do it'. Are human beings mammals with an autonomous consciousness; authors of our present and future experience? Or is it the case that freewill is like an optical illusion of consciousness making our present, and therefore our future predetermined by our biology and personal history?

The advent of the genome project has given rise to numerous reports in the media that the discovery of a particular gene is a determinant of specific behavioural tendencies or orientations of character. Articles such as 'Middle-class children have better genes, says former schools chief... and we just have to accept it' (Clark, 2009), have become common in the British popular press. If such reports were to form the cornerstone of a belief system, one may be drawn to conclude that genes are destiny. However, other fields of research, such as complexity theory and the technical advances in affective neuroscience provide alternative lenses to the prism of understanding the human condition, suggesting that ontological stages of development may be adaptive.

It is the intention of this paper to explore these issues which may have an implicit, or explicit relevance in the personal and social arenas of human relationships, initially by surveying the literature of affective neuroscience, complexity theory and epigentics. The final part of the paper will take the form of an appraisal of the study, which will include references to a small scale sample of psycho-social research, previously undertaken in preliminary modules of this MSc. In addition, there will be a reflexive element in the closing sections of the paper drawing upon my personal experience as an adult with a form of autism known as Asperger's Syndrome. These issues surrounding the dualism of nature or nurture, fatalism or a Platonic opportunity to negotiate the determinism of my autistic spectrum orientation are brought into sharp focus; I shall recount my lifelong attempts to transform my Asperger's, dyslexic and dyspraxic fate into an adaptive creative process in which I can not only manage daily life as an adult, but also endeavour to thrive and aspire to excellence.

Affective Neuroscience:

Affective neuroscience is an emerging discipline, exploring the neurobiology of emotions (Watt, 2003, p. 79). Panksepp suggests that a neurological understanding of the basic operations of the mammalian brain may provide a unifying understanding between different approaches to the human condition and psychology; such as ethology, behaviourism and the cognitive sciences (Panksepp, 2005, p. 5). A tenet of affective neuroscience is the role that emotions and subjective experience play in the causal chain of events which control action, and these arise from neurobiological events which regulate and modulate instincts and experience (Panksepp, 2005, p. 14). This approach contrasts the materialistic view that mind and body are distinct and different (Edelman and Tonino, 2000, p. 4), and that there is a mini self within the self; a homunculus which perceives sensory afferent data, such as visual signals, as if on a mini screen within the mind, like a watching a screen in a theatre (Koch, 2004, p. 298). Domasio has described what is known as the 'dualism of the Cartesian theatre' as, 'Descarte's error,' suggesting that mind and body share a relationship from which subjective experience emerges (Domasio, 1995, p. 250). Neuroscience has recently begun to direct its attention away from anatomy-as-causality towards a systems orientated approach between body and brain (Corrigal and Wilkinson, 2003, p.1). However, in *The Master and his Emissary*, McGilchrist suggests that the architecture of the brain is akin to the architecture of how we construct experience (McGilchrist, 2009, p. 7), and it is to the development of the brain that investigation of determinism and agency in affective neuroscience begins its journey.

Determinism: an innate predisposition of nature

To approach this investigation of how character and personal expression may be predetermined this paper will consider three different models: genetics, neuroscience and complexity theory.

Genetic science has blossomed since the early 1990s and provided an understanding of biological causality in human behaviour (Fonagay et al, 2004, p. 103). Genetic determinism holds the view that all behavioural responses, traits and characteristics can be located in a correlating genotype, while the environment is perceived as a passive agent and it is one's genes which influence the responses to independent or environmental variables (Fonagay et al, 2004, p. 105). It is perhaps temping to adopt the reductive view that genes somehow correlate with destiny (Lipton, 2005, p. 37), and that all biological processes can be explained in terms of molecular functions and mechanisms (Capra, 1996, p. 77). Genetic science is far more complex than the simplistic notion that a single gene correlates with a specific character trait. However, the 'Primacy of DNA' model suggests a genetic determinism; a first cause in the construction of protein (Lipton, 20005 p. 31). Genes though, are not static units of physical hereditary; there are different classes of gene, and these have a number of adaptive functions throughout the life cycle (Lloyd and Rossi, 1992, p. 404).

During the first four months of gestation in the womb, there is a heightened production of neurons in the embryo's developing brain (Dowling, 2004, p. 10). Postnataly, the brain continues to develop in spurts of critical growth activity (Schore, 2003, p.131), and virtually all neurons are developed by 6 months after birth (Dowling, 2004, p. 10). The maturation of the prefrontal cortex is postnatal (Schore, 1994, p. 13). During the first two years of life, critical periods of growth occur mostly in the right brain (Cozolino, 2006, p.38). During infancy the increase in brain size is due to the growth and elaboration of neurons; not only do the cells grow but they also extend more dendritic branches. It is estimated that in excess of 80 % of dendritic growth occurs after birth. It is on the dendrites of a neuron that synaptic contacts are made and this early period ushers an enormous increase in the synaptic circuitry of the brain (Dowling, 2004, p. 10). There is a substantial rearrangement and pruning of synapses during brain development and growth; not only are new synaptic connections added, but many others are lost. The highest quantity of synaptic connections reaches a peak between six to eight months after birth, and then total numbers begin to decline (Dowling, 2004, p. 13).

Glaser reports that the stepwise development of the brain is genetically predetermined and cannot be modified or altered by either experience or the environment (Glaser, 2003, p. 119). Neuron growth is followed by a period of synaptic networking. Sensory centres serving both vision and hearing are the earliest to mature, in sequence which continues until late adolescence. Glucose is a primary energy source for neurons which increase their demand with activity. In newborns, glucose utilization is largely limited to the brain stem, parts of the cerebrum and some subcortical structures. By two to three months of age, glucose utilization increases significantly, especially in the occipital cortex; the area concerned with visual processing and perception. Glucose utilization reaches a peak between four and seven years of age, at which point it is used at almost twice the rate than that of the adult brain. The peaking of glucose consumption appears to relate to the abundant synaptic plasticity during this period (Dowling, 2004, p. 14). Schore reports that there are a number of biochemical differences between an immature and mature brain. The metabolic changes which result in higher energy output allow for an increasing complexity of structure and integration. This stepwise maturation represents an experiential shaping of genetic potential. Genes do not exert their total influence at birth, but are amplified during the progressive stages of maturation (Schore, 1994, p. 16). Neurochemical systems develop and re-mould at both pre- and post-synaptic sites throughout the lifespan. Receptor fields proliferate and diminish during different phases of ontological development and neurons in motivational systems can expand or shrink (Panksepp, 2005, p. 59).

The brain changes throughout the lifespan, growing rapidly at the start of life and reaches its maximum weight around the age of twenty. By the age of fifty, the size of the brain begins to alter in the opposite direction and reduces in size. Dowling suggests brain shrinkage may be as much as 15% over a lifespan of one hundred years. Neuronal atrophy; a loss of white matter and the possible degeneration of mylene sheaths which surround axons, contributes to a loss of neural efficiency (Dowling, 2004, p. 141). At the time of birth, the infant's brain already has a certain architecture, suggesting a predisposition to perceive, comprehend and behave in specific ways. Changes to the architecture of the brain may also correlate with changes in perception, response, and personality. The relationship between mind and brain has been more deeply understood with the advancement of technology. Panksepp reports that a central assumption of neuroscience is that all psychological functions ultimately emerge from the workings of the brain; memories, emotions, motivations and the mind are all dependant on the network of structures and the architecture of this vital organ (Panksepp, 2005, p. 59).

In *The Web of Life*, Fritjof Capra illustrates how complexity theory has transformed the field of biology from a mechanistic model towards systems thinking (Capra, 1996, p. 29). From a systems perspective, an organism may be thought of both as an embodied object made of components; a structure, and also as a process or pattern in which the organism is understood not as a set of components, but rather as a qualitive relationship between the component parts (Capra, 1996, p. 81). Through the lens of complexity theory, organisms are viewed as systems of self regeneration though a process known as autopiesis (Capra, 1996, p. 29). Capra writes:

> *Auto*, of course, means 'self' and refers to the
> autonomy of self-organizing systems; and *poiesis*
> - which shares the same Greek root as the word
> 'poetry' – means 'making'. So, autopiesis means
> 'self-making'. (Capra, 1996, p. 97).

An autopietic system is one in which a network of production processes whereby the function of each component participates in the production or transformation of other components in the network (Capra, 1996, p. 98). Capra identifies the key criteria of a living system, stating that the configuration of relational processes; dissipating structures within a network of feedback loops, determine a system's essential characteristics. The structure is the physical embodiment of the system's pattern of organization, while its life process is the activity involved in the continual embodiment of the system's pattern of organization (Capra, 1996, p. 98).

A cell is bounded by a membrane, which is formed by some of the cell's components. The membrane both encloses the network of the cell's metabolic processes and actively participates in the maintenance of the network by selecting raw material for the production processes such as drawing food from the environment, whilst also dissipating waste into the environment. 'Thus, the autopietic network creates its own boundary, which defines the cell as a distinct living system while being an active part of the network'. (Capra, 1996, p. 163). Viewing an organism as a non-linear dynamical system has bought a new understanding of life to the field of biology. The multi-cellular human body is not a static object, but rather, it is a dynamic system in a constant state of flux and change. Its stability is maintained by remaining far from equilibrium, dissipating and re-organizing itself in an ongoing process of life (Capra, 1996, p. 175). A useful metaphor is that of a whirlpool in a fast flowing river. A structure emerges within the fast flowing water, the shape of which is maintained by the constant flow. Each molecule of the whirlpool is constantly replaced, and it is this replacement of particles which maintains the system. The dynamic process of breakdown and renewal is consistent in all life forms, maintaining the overall identity or pattern of organisation. In the human body, the pancreas replaces its cells every twenty four hours, the lining of the stomach, once every three days, and the skin replaces its cells at the rate of 100,000 cells per minute; ninety-eight percent of the protein in the brain is replaced every month (Capra, 1996, p. 213).

Complexity theory shows that organisms do not just exist within their environment; the environment plays a key role in maintaining the structure and life of the organism. Networks of living systems are nested within their surroundings, forming complex organisms, eco-systems and societies, all of which are autopietic networks (Capra, 1996, p. 204). The human social network is both biological and conceptual. Language forms an organized conceptual system within closed social groups which operate autopietically (Capra, 1996, p. 207). Within a family system, conversations can exhibit inherent circularities, which give rise to further conversations, creating feedback loops and closed systems of meaning. Social discourses provide a context within which the meaning attributed to text or verbal language may be distinctly perceived (Fairclough, 1992, p.79). In *The Selfish Gene*, Dawkins defines inherited cultural discourse, carried by units of cultural transmission or imitation, as a 'meme' (Dawkins, 2006, p. 193). Writers of evolutionary psychology agree that genetic and cultural processes operate in similar ways and yet have unique properties which influence the phenotype in different ways (Laland and Brown, 2002, p. 275). An example might be drawn between

140

the more commonly known form of natural selection, the survival of the fittest; survival and protection from predation, and sexual selection which may have cultural implications and may even risk the initial survival impulse. For example the peacock's tail has adapted to serve reproduction and yet it disadvantageously inhibits flight and increases the risk of predation (Barrett et al, 2002, p. 359). At this stage of the investigation that it would appear to be the case that context plays a role in the orientation of development. An autopietic system; a cell, is nested within a body, which itself is nested within a family situated in a social culture (Glaser, 2003, 117). Ultimately, these nested environments are themselves nested within the autopietic system of the earth's ecology and perhaps the even solar system (Capra, 1996, p. 211).

At this stage of the investigation, the findings may seem conclusive. The primacy model of DNA shows that the human genome contains the blue-print of all the potentials of what we may become. The human organism is an autopietic system, engaged in a continuous flow of self-organisation and re-creation. Brain maturation follows a sequence of bursts of neural growth, which are known as critical or sensitive periods. During these periods the architecture of the brain is adapted and modified, which suggests that the synaptic networks of our perceptions, thoughts and character are moulded by our biology. If the investigation stopped at this point, it would seem natural to form the conclusion that whatever we may become is determined by nature alone, and we are held in the fate of a bio-causality. However, the findings also show that the ontology of development has a step-wise process which allows the genetic potentials to be read and engaged within a temporal context and the quality of each stage is dependent upon the experience of preceding stages. Although it appears that an individual's trajectory is determined by how experiences interact with time, it may be premature to form any conclusions before the role of space is considered. The study will now investigate the role of the environment in determinism.

The role of the environment in determinism:

It has been shown in this study that context plays a role in the orientation and development of experience, but is the environment also a factor in the development of content?

The theory of dissipative structures shows that autopietic systems introject the environment in which they are nested. The structure of the self is regulated and maintained by remaining far from equilibrium. This state is, however, not one of passive introjection; it is both introjective and intrajective and produces points of instability in which dramatic and unpredictable events may take place. It is from these points that order spontaneously emerges and complexity unfolds. Bifurcation describes the process of how a dissipative structure, at a point of threshold, may either break down or break through to one of several new states of order. Capra reports that what happens at a bifurcation point depends upon the system's prior history and states, 'Depending on which path it has taken to reach the point of instability, it will follow one or another of the available branches after the bifurcation', Capra, 1996, p. 186). Living structure is a record of previous development, with the present structure determined by its history. In addition to the self replicating cyclic transformations that occur within a living system which serve to maintain the structure of the system in a status quo, a type of change may also take place in which new structures, or new connections within the autopietic network are created. The term structural coupling describes the interaction of a system with its environment. Inanimate objects react to environmental events with predictable linearity. However, in non-linear dynamical systems, an autopietic system will respond, rather than merely react (Capra, 1996, p. 214). Etymologically, the word development means to unwrap or unfold, suggesting a logical, sequential trajectory of potentiality (Geert, 2009, p. 248). Over the entire lifespan of a human being, changes may occur via biologically governed processes and also by learning. This may be done by appropriating and assimilating new knowledge and niche-seeking, or niche construction in which an organism may move toward or even create environments which optimally fit its properties (Geert, 2009, p. 249). However, all changes of the system occur through information which is moderated through the system. Actions which initiate short term processes of moderation within the system interrelate with long-term ontological potentials and alter the parameters and properties that constitute the long-term ensemble of development (Geert, 2009, p. 249). Complexity theory shows that stages of development, or phase transitions, have non-linear dynamical properties which operate like continuous, and dis-continuous, attractors. When a system reaches a tipping point, cascades of change induce bifurcations in the orientation or trajectory of perception or behaviour which then informs the quality of the next stage or phase. The brain's plasticity and its ability to be shaped by experience, facilitates further adaptation and assimilation of new experiences (Geert, 2009, p. 270).

These findings show that the environment plays a role at the cellular level in the both the form and trajectory of an organism's development. It would appear to be the case that human experience is determined by the relationship between pre-dispositions held within the innate gene potentials and the physical environment in which the person grows. However, people are social beings and the next stage of the study will investigate the emotional and psychological role of the relational environment.

The nurturing of nature: the predisposition of a relational self:

The pattern in complexity theory, showing how the present is determined by the quality of past experience in an organism's history, is also observed in affective neuroscience. Glaser asserts that while the sequence of the stepwise development of the brain is genetically predetermined and cannot be altered by environment and experience; the quality of each stage is influenced by the experience of those which precede it; the nature of what has previously been learned will shape and direct the orientation of subsequent learning (Glaser, 2003, p. 123).

It is not just on a cellular level that the human organism is receptive to its environment. Studies show that the environment draws salient properties of gene expression to the fore. Schore reports that that early postnatal development represents an experiential shaping of genetic potential. Genetic effects do not exert their total influence at birth, but are amplified during periods of stepwise maturational progressions of development. Different and specific gene-environment interactions are thought to occur over the course of development. Increased levels of both brain DNA and RNA synthesis continue from birth through the second year: the human cerebral cortex adds about 70% of its final DNA content after birth. In addition, in the postnatal expanding brain, the diversity of RNA sequences and the amount of protein are directly influenced by early environmental enrichment and social isolation experiences (Schore, 1994, p. 16).

A field of biological study known as Epigenetics, meaning, 'control above genetics', suggests that DNA blueprints passed down through genes are not rigorously defined at birth. Environmental influences, including nutrition, stress, and emotions, can modify those genes without changing their basic blueprint (Lipton, 2005, p. 36). This paper has shown that an organism is comprised of both structure and process. The structure of a gene is its DNA. The active, or inactive, expression of the gene is its ongoing process. Chromosomal proteins play a crucial role in hereditary, along with DNA. These proteins cover the DNA core like a sleeve, preventing that genetic material from being read (Lipton, 2005, p. 37). Another class of genes, sometimes referred to as 'immediate-early genes', 'primary response genes', or 'third messengers', are actively turned on or off in response to physical and psychosocial stimuli. Rossi asserts that a wide range of events in the environment, ranging from physical trauma, temperature, food, sexual stimuli and novelty can activate neurons where immediate-early genes are turned on to initiate the arousal of creative response systems at the molecular-genetic level (Rossi, 2000, p. 179). Inter mediate-early genes do not require full cycles of fresh protein synthesis for their expression and can be activated immediately; from within seconds to a minute or two, playing a key role in mediating psychological arousal and optimal performance as well as the stress response (Rossi, 2002, p.13).

These findings show an interplay between gene expression and environment. From the moment of birth, both the environment and early social experiences influence which genetic potentials unfold, prompting biologists such as Lipton to describe parents as 'genetic engineers' (Lipton, 2005, p. 125). A process known as genetic transcription is a secondary level of genetic involvement in the brain's development. Transcription genes control the experience-dependant aspects of the brain's organisation and development by allowing the brain to be shaped and re-shaped by learning. Cozolino concurs with Schore, reporting that the transcription of protein into neural structure via RNA, is a growth process of learning and adaptation. He concludes, 'Thus, nature and nurture contribute to the building of the brain via the template and transcription function of our genes', (Cozolino, 2006, p. 40).

Similar findings are evident in neuroscience; neural growth and synaptic networks are influenced and shaped by experience and the environment. Brain development occurs during periods of exuberant neural growth and connectivity, known as critical or sensitive periods. Research shows that the timing of these periods is not determined by genes alone; it is also influenced by both experience and the nature of what is being learned, (Cozolino, 2002, p. 780.

Dowling asserts that experience plays a critical role in the maturation of brain circuitry (Dowling, 2004, P. 33). As neural networks are formed, they group together and are either strengthened and sustained by repeated usage, or weakened and diminished by lack of activity (Valera et al, 1993, p. 87). Edelman and Tononi state, 'Neurons that wire together, fire together', and a form of selectionism takes place (Edelman and Tononi, 2000, p. 83). The extent of neuronal cell death varies in different brain regions. The cerebral cortex undergoes little neuronal degeneration, whereas the spinal cord and some regions of the hindbrain may lose between 30 % and 75 % of their neurons during the maturation of the central nervous system. During brain maturation there is a rearrangement and refinement of synapses and axonal terminal fields. Newly formed neurons extend their branches over a wider area during maturation. In the process of networks becoming established, some of both the axonal branches and synapses are lost, while others are formed. Innervation of muscles and neurons takes place at birth, as innervate muscle fibres and autonomic ganglion cell neurons stimulate the regulation of internal organs (Dowling, 2004, P. 34). The underlying process behind cell loss and rearrangement of synapses is chemically mediated. Key proteins in this process are neurotrophins, which regulate cell death, dendritic and axonal branching and the extent and pattern of synaptic innervations. Dowling reports,

> Both presynaptic and postsynaptic neurons, as well as some glial cells, are known to release neurotrophins. Neuro-trophins interact with specific membrane proteins, called Trk (ty-rosine kinase-containing) receptors. These receptor proteins extend across the membrane with the portion on the outside of the cell available for neurotrophin binding, whereas the part inside the cell acts as a kinase enzyme. The binding of a neurotrophin molecule to a Trk receptor protein activates the kinase and initiates a series of intracellular biochemical reactions. These biochemical events within the cell can alter enzyme activity and gene expression. (Dowling, 2004, P. 34).

Dowling asserts that the chemical process which drives the selectionism of neural networks is triggered by environmental factors and experience and the most ideal area in which to observe the maturation process is the visual system, which are easily recorded (Dowling, 2004, p. 53). Visual information is first processed in the cortex and is highly selective in orientation, responding to stimuli which is moving and presented at a certain angle. When visual neurons are shown a light bar which is orientated more than 10% from optimum receptivity, the response of neuron cells is diminished. Deeper into the network, further away from the input source, cortex cells have even stricter requirements if they are to be activated; with orientation and movement playing a role in the stimulation of these complex neural groups. These findings suggest that the neuronal machinery is not present at birth, but develops in response to the visual environment. Experiments in visual deprivation with cats and rats show that monocular deprivation; the covering of one eye, directly affects the development of neural cells, altering both the strength and pattern of the network. These experiments showed that; more neurons had established themselves in the region behind the open eye. In visual enriched conditions, the number of synapses per neuron in the optical cortex of rats increased by 20% to 25 %; the weight of the cortex increased along with the ratio of synapses per neuron. The conclusion drawn from these studies is that enriched environments increase neuronal size, glial cell growth, synaptic density per neuron, and synaptic size. From birth, an initial over production of neurons in a developing brain is then pruned through maturation by intrinsic experience-based factors which sculpt the architecture of the brain (Dowling, 2004, P. 56).

Studies in newborn consciousness show that a newborn infant does not just conceive solid continuous objects, concave spaces, physical motions and pattern changes. They also display a particular sensitivity to stimuli from people and are able to identify a caregiver. Innate skills include grasping hold of the mother, orienting to and from her breast and recognising her odour and voice. Trevarthen and Reddy report that within a few hours after birth a baby looks longer at a mother's face than that of a stranger, even when all other sensory cues are excluded (Trevarthen and Reddy, 2007, p. 45). Schore states that the gaze held between a mother and infant is important not just for recognition, but it also plays an key role of the regulation of the homeostasis of the system (Schore, 1994, p. 97). In addition to the heat exchange of skin contact which helps the infant's hypothalamus to establish and regulate body temperature (Cozolino, 2006, p. 102), the mutual gaze between the infant and mother creates a symbiotic psychobiological state in which the adult and infant's homeostatic states are linked together super-ordinate organisation which allows for the mutual regulation of autonomic, endocrine and central nervous systems (Schore, 1994, p. 78). The relationship between a mother and newborn infant is one of mutual communication, in which a continual adjustment to one another's sounds, gestures and movements occur in what Cozolino describes as a lyrical duet. 'As they bond, both of their brains are shaped and reshaped in response to one another', (Cozolino, 2006, p. 97). Trevarthen concurs, suggesting that the dyadic relationship has a sense of musicality in which either the infant or the mother may play the role of conductor (Trevarthen, 2003, p.73). Studies have shown that as early as three months old, an infant displays anticipatory behaviours and responses and invites imitation in the care giver. The exchange becomes a dialogue animated by the adult's anticipation and pleasure and by the infant's emotions: the pulse of the baby's heart accelerates just before the baby imitates a movement, but slows when the baby is about to provocate. Trevarthern later reports with Reddy that by six weeks, the infant responds to contingent human signals with smiles, hand gestures and cooing in the first proto-conversations. The infant shares rhythms of address and reply, and the affectionate talk of a parent that pleases a young baby has a structure found in the basis of music or poetry (Trevarthen and Reddy, 2009, p. 46). Schore asserts that for the developing infant, the mother is the environment (Schore, 1994, p. 78) and this dyadic relationship is vital for learning to regulate affect during key stages in ontogenetic adaptation (Schore, 1994, p. 18).

Affect is a term borrowed from German psychological usage (Laplanche and Pontalis, 1973, p. 13), and describes an independent pattern of sensory input which forms the pre-conscious basis of the experience of emotion before it is distilled into a cognitive awareness of feeling (Folezbee, 2007, p.42). Panksepp suggests that emotional abilities initially emerge from instinctual operating systems of the brain, which allow animals to begin gathering food, information and other resources needed to sustain life. Emotive systems undergo refinement in higher brain areas as they mature and organisms make effective behavioural choices. Emotional tendencies such as those related to fear, anger and separation-distress emerge during early developmental stages, providing coping strategies for dealing with emergencies which might compromise survival. Other emotional systems such as seeking, play, nurturance and sexuality have a role in establishing and maintaining social structures which may in turn influence propagation (Panksepp, 2005, p. 26). Primary affective states may have evolved to facilitate rapid adaptive responses to phenomena by learned association and emotional arousal which form a gestalt mood to prompt specific behaviour. In *Affective Consciousness*, Panksepp writes;

At minimum, affective consciousness can be parsed into at least three general varieties: (i) the exteroceptively driven *sensory-affects* that reflect the pleasures and aversions of worldly objects and events; (ii) the interoceptively driven *homeostatic-affects,* such as hunger and thirst, that reflect the states of the peripheral body along the continuum of survival, and (iii) the *emotional-affects* that reflect the arousal of brain instinctual action systems that are built into sub-neocortical regions of the brain as basic tools for living – to respond to major life challenges such as various life-threatening stimuli (leading to fear, anger, and separation-distress) and the search for various life-supporting stimuli and interactions (reflected in species-typical seeking and playfulness, as well as socio-sexual eagerness and maternal care), (Panksepp, 2008, p.115).

Fonagy et al, report that classical psychoanalysis and attachment theory view affects in distinctly different ways (Fonagy et al, 2004, p. 94). The former approaches affects as a unitary phenomenon of drives and primitive powerful forces, which may be categorised as positive or negative, both of which may be considered to be of value in certain contexts. In contrast, attachment theorists approach affects from a systems perspective, viewing the interrelation of affects as a heterogeneous process of regulation. This approach also encapsulates the psycho-social perspective of viewing the individual as a situated part of a relational whole. Affect regulation is an embodied system which functions in a similar way to the homeostasis, arousing or deactivating affects in response to experience.

Shore reports that the dyadic interaction between the newborn and primary carer modulates and controls the infant's homeostasis and that, '... attachment theory is fundamentally a regulatory theory' (Shore, 2003, p118). Of special importance is the mother's participation in the reparation dynamics of reunion. Secure attachment facilitates the transfer of regulatory capacities from caregiver to infant (Schore, 1994, p.31). Cozolino asserts that, 'attachment schemas reflect the transduction of interpersonal experience into the biological structure', the dynamics of the affective experience correlate with linkages of the orbital medial prefrontal cortex and the amygdala with the regulatory systems (Cozolino, 2006, p. 146). The deactivation of affective arousal can be mediated by reunion with an attachment figure, most usually the mother. Shore attests that reunion behaviour is more indicative of the quality of attachment than, for example, a child's protests at a point of separation (Shore, 1994, p.100). Reunion transactions with the attuned caregiver maintain the arousal level; an infant's reentering into patterned interactive states with the caregiver regulates the arousal, affective and attention states of the infant. This is mediated by visual contact with the mother, or care giver (Cozolino, 2006, p. 101). In addition, Score reports that an epigenetic sequence of adaptive issues is negotiated by the caregiver-infant dyad towards achieving self-regulation (Schore, 1994, p.31). He continues;

> Visual stimulation, embedded in mutual gaze transactions between caregiver and infant, is an essential component of a growth promoting environment. The moth¬er's emotionally expressive face is the most potent source of visuoaffective information, and in face-to-face interactions it serves as a visual imprinting stimulus for the infant's developing nervous system. During visual dialogues the primary caregiver is psychobiologically attuned to the infant's internal state, and in these merger experiences she creates and maintains a mutually regulated symbiotic state in the dyad.

These findings from the field of affective neuroscience describe the mechanism of how the environment is introjected and influences the inner landscape of the emergent psyche of the infant. This is then intrajected and mirrored by the mother. Bion postulates the concept of the maternal container, whose capacity for reverie transforms the unpleasant sensations (Fonagat et al, 2004, p. 191). Schore describes this process in further detail:

> In mirroring transactions, a dyadic reciprocal stimulating system generates an elevation of regulated sympathetic

arousal that supports heightened levels of interest-excitement and enjoyment-joy. This amplification of positive affect is neurochemically mediated by activation of the ventral tegmental dopa-minergic system and the stimulation of endogenous opioids in reward centers of the infant's brain. The child's capacity to tolerate higher levels of arousal increases over the first year. These phenomena culminate in very high levels of positive affect at the onset of the practicing phase at the end of the first year. (Schore, 1994, p.91).

Panksepp concurs, writing, 'The first neurochemical system that was found to exert a powerful inhibitory effect on separation distress was the opioid system. This provided a powerful new way to understand social attachments (Panksepp, 2005, p.255). During social interactions, opioids are released in the brain, prompting sensations of pleasure. Bowlby first identified the attachment schema, stating that ethology studies have shown the need for a secure base is ubiquitous in nature. (Bowlby, 1988, p.33). A secure base acts like the sanctuary from which explorations into the world can be launched and into which one can return for safety (Bowlby, 1979, p.125). All affectionate bonds are ruptured during the course of ordinary living (Bowlby, 1979, p.86). It is the quality of reparation, satisfactory or otherwise, which forms the basis of a particular style of response to anxiety when security is threatened (Cozolino, 2006, p. 140). These responsive styles are known as attachment behaviours (Bowlby, 1988, p.31). There are three main types of behaviour triggered by the arousal of the attachment system, one of which may be viewed in polarity (Cozolino, 2006, p. 141).

- Secure Attachment

- Insecure attachment type one: Avoidant Attachment

- Insecure Attachment type two: Ambivalent Attachment

- Disorganised Attachment

A number of neurochemicals play a key role in mediating separation and reunion; AVP, oxytocin and the opioid systems are prime movers in the construction and maintenance of social bonds in mammals ((Panksepp, 2005, p.256). The release or inhibition of these chemicals prompt social behaviours such as seeking and the reparation of separation distress, and during critical periods of brain maturation these may become imprinted into the limbic structures (Schore, 1994, p. 114). Cozolino reports that although the brain is capable of social adaptation throughout the life span, attachment patterns are apparent by the end of the first year of life. The neurochemical responses formed during critical periods engenders a strength of learning which results in early experiences having a disproportionately powerful role in sculpting the networks of attachment and affect regulation (Cozolino, 2002, p. 179). The mechanism of imprinting; a rapid form of learning which forms the basis of attachment bond formation, has been considered to involve an irreversible stamping of early experience upon the developing nervous system (Schore, 1994, p. 116). This is sometimes referred to as 'template learning' whereby a gestalt of emotional and affective states becomes neurologically associated with dyadic experiences that are embedded into the maternal-infant gaze transactions, which become networked among sequential stimuli and behaviour. The orbitofrontal cortex contains neurons which track emotionally relevant objects in interpersonal space and respond to the expressions on faces. During the episodes of visuoaffective nervous system entraining, this region is exposed to the mother's frontolimbic cortex via her eye and head movements together with facial and motor responses implicated in her behaviour, which serve as a template for the structural imprinting of the infant's orbitofrontal cortex and its function in attachment processes (Schore, 1994, p. 116). The arousal of the maternal socioaffective stimulation emulating from the mother's emotionally expressive face induces high levels of arousal in the infant, which in turn promotes the imprinting of new circuits in the orbitofrontal cortex. Subsequently, this induces the experience-dependant sprouting of dopamine-releasing axon varicosites in the deep layers of the prefrontal cortex. This prompts a growth spurt in the blood vessels, neurons, and glia of the prefrontal cortex, and more so in the early maturing right hemisphere (Schore, 1994, p. 134).

Findings from the field of affective neuroscience show that the environment, and specifically the maternal socioaffective environment, play a key role in determining the formation and architecture of the brain. When a neural pathway is activated by a stimulus, the synapses which are engaged store a chemical signal, and the repetition of the stimuli stabilizes the neural pattern, which becomes less susceptible to change. The instruction to attend to the caregiver is genetic, and the quality and content of neural growth and formation of implicit memory is determined by the quality and content of interactions with the primary caregivers (Glaser, 2000, p. 121). Because the imprinting and implicit early learning is essentially unconscious, it has the additional power of organizing our background affect, our views of the world and our relationships prior to the development of conscious awareness. Early suboptimal experiences of bonding and attachment become imprinted within the social circuits of the brain and are carried into adulthood (Cozolino, 2002, p. 179). Shore's findings show that the psychobiological attunement of attachment occurs in relationships throughout the lifespan. The operation of the attachment dynamic continues during adulthood and the activation of an internal system, first developed with the primary carer, maintains an affective state of enjoyment and well being (Shore, 1994, p. 107). Kirkpatrick reports there are parallels between infant-mother interactions and those between adult lovers; prolonged eye contact, cooing or talking "baby talk," and other intimate behaviours are similar to those displayed by infants to elicit and maintain contact with an attachment figure (Kirkpatrick, 2005 p 40).

At this stage of the investigation, it would appear to be conclusive that perception, behaviour and character are determined. While the concept of determinism can be misconstrued as a form of bio-causality which may become used for manipulative political purposes, of which Nazi Germany is a clear example (Pinker, 2002, p. 180). Pinker suggests that determinism does not abnegate personal responsibility for one's actions, stating it is an error to confuse explanation with exculpation (Pinker, 2002 p. 179). Sheldrake proposes that determinism can only be viewed as probability and that there is most likely a gradient of determinism, suggesting that, 'The immediate future is more determined than the remote future' (Sheldrake, 2003, p. 265).

This paper has shown that the genetic coding of our biology is part of a self-oganising system which self-replicates and maintains its structures through the process of autopiesis. In addition, the paper shows that genes are epigenetic in nature and salient potentials emerge as a direct result of interaction with the environment. The dyadic relationship sculpts the formation of neural networks and controls the regulation of affect. Visuoaffective gaze transactions stimulate further cortical development and become imprinted into the embedded nervous system and form the basis of attachment bonding responses. This being the case, the question arises as to whether we are bound to constantly re-live constructs of our past, doomed to be nothing more than an echo of our history.

Adult brain development and neural plasticity:

It has been shown in this paper that experience influences the rewiring of brain synapses. However, the rewiring of synaptic connections is not just limited to young brains. Sensitive, or critical periods create optimal learning periods for the developing brain. Glaser asserts that the acquisition of language, for example, is more easily assimilated in early development and experience-dependant processes continue to generate new synaptic development into adulthood. He remarks, 'The Brain's ability to change its own structure in response to the environment and experience is termed neuroplasticity' (Glaser, 2003, p. 122). The maturing brain reaches its maximum weight around the age of twenty (Dowling, 2004, p. 10). From the onset of puberty, further ontological stages occur as the brain undergoes a process of disorganization and reorganization. The process of step-wise development continues as natural developmental milestones and life challenges coincide with periods of neural development and enhanced plasticity (Cozolino, 2006, p. 44). The last brain structure to mature is the cerebral cortex; the seat of higher mental functions, such as perception, explicit memory, judgement and reasoning. These vertical areas do not mature simultaneously; those concerned with sensory processing mature in advance of those which deal with planning, intentionality and other aspects of the personality. These areas are still myelinating axons and rearranging synapses into early adulthood at around the age of eighteen (Dowling, 2004, p. 13). Cozolino also reports that during the period between the ages of twelve to eighteen, the overall number of neurons, otherwise known as grey matter, diminishes while the white matter, comprising myelinated fibres which connect functional neural networks, increases . This suggests a continuation of the selectional process which may have an evolutionary agenda to promote faster and more efficient information processing. 'Enhanced efficiency and speed of communication among cortical areas and between cortical and subcortical structures ultimately leads to increased integration of brain functions located in diverse regions of the central nervous system' (Cozolino, 2006, p. 44).

The connectivity between neurons increases into mid-life and then begins to decline. While this may sound alarming, apoptosis occurs as a part of the brain's earlier development and correlates with increased functioning. This later period of neural reorganization correlates with a simultaneous utilization of both hemispheres in processing information. The bi-lateral processing of the aging brain may be cognitively slower but suggests a wisdom that is derived from the hemispheric specialization which is acquired from the development of specific skill building (Cozolino, 2000, p. 46).

The literature surveyed in this paper shows that throughout the entire lifespan the brain has the potential to be changed by our experiences, and these changes are reflected in the synaptic circuitry of the brain (Dowling, 2004, p. 13). In *The Psychobiology of Gene Expression*, Rossi reports that neuroscientists are investigating how novelty, environment enrichment and voluntary acts of physical exercise can modulate gene expression to encode new memory and learning. Activity dependant gene expression is associated with motivation and with conscious experiences of numinosity, such as music, wonder, fantasy, art, mystery and creative daydreaming. He proposes that a function of cultural experience is to turn on activity dependant gene expression which facilitates neurogenesis and the growth of the brain (Rossi, 2002, p.12). Geert also proposes that human development occurs over the lifespan, stating that the complex and non-linear dynamical system of a human being is recursive and self organising, involving many levels and layers of nested organization. These include the individual person who is situated among their interactions with others, institutions and cultures to which the person relates (Geert, 2009, p. 271). Bifurcation points of development are reached in both continuous and discontinuous forms, and these temporal points of phase transition are mediated by both domain and context (Geert, 2009, p. 260).

While neural plasticity and perspectives from complexity theory present viable arguments against the case for a rigid determinism, the role of the environment in both the maintenance and transformation of the structures which contain experience appears to remain unassailed at this stage of the investigation. In *Affect Dysregulation and Disorders of the Self*, Schore comments that the environment only determines psychological residuals of development such as habits and memories, while brain maturation occurs on a fixed ontological calendar. He states, 'Environmental experience is now recognized to be critical to the differentiation of brain tissue itself. 'Nature's potential can be realized only as it is enabled by nurture' (Schore, 2003, p. 73).

The environment of a single cell is contained by a permeable midbrain which maintains its structure by allowing for a continual flow of substances to cross its threshold, both inwardly and outwardly. In a

158

similar fashion, if one views the home as a container for human experience, this too has a bounded and permeable threshold. The home can represent a variety of polarities, such as a refuge or safe haven or domain for violence; dirt exists outside the house but may be brought inside by muddy feet, while the waste products of life within the home are removed and placed in the external environment (Sibley, 1995, p. 94). The dividing lines between apparent spatial and psychological polarities such as communal areas or private space, or inside and outside, may be illusionary from the systems' perspective of the self as a relational being.

Klein proposed the theory of the mother-as-container which was further developed by Bion as container-contained (Hinshelwood, 1989, p. 249). Affective neuroscience supports this perspective and provides deeper insights into the mechanisms of the socio-emotive imprinting. The arousal regulating transactions of synchrony and asynchrony of a mother's attunement to the infant's affective states as bonds are formed, broken and repaired are downloaded into the early imagistic, visceral and nonverbal implicit-procedural memory system of the right brain (Schore, 2003, p. 79). Dysregulation of affect may result from instances of neglect or a failure of environmental stimulation during critical periods of brain development (Glaser, 2003, p. 123). Glaser states that disorganized attachment is believed to be both an infant and young child's response to an attachment figure who is the cause of distress, either by reacting angrily towards the child, or by withdrawing. Children who experience compulsive-punitive dyadic relationships display problems in their school years, and may experience emotional and behavioural difficulties in adolescence as a result of a maladaptive process of development (Glaser, 2003, p. 129).

In the light of these findings which suggest a psychopathological determinism, the prospect of generating new experiences carries with it the necessity for the reduction or elimination of distress and emotional pain. In view of this, the innate capability of the brain to restructure and reorganise itself during sensitive periods throughout the lifespan prompts a further question; is it possible for an individual with a maladapted imprinting of affect dysregulation or insecure attachment responses to deliberately induce the bifurcation of new patterns of secure attachment or productive, healthy and life enhancing forms of affect regulation by placing themselves in an environment of care which is co-created for the purpose of nurturing resolution and transformation?

159

Finding new pathways in the therapeutic environment:

Affect, both its regulation and dysregulation, plays an important role in the infant-caregiver and patient-therapist relationship (Schore, 2003, p. 63). Affective neuroscience has illuminated the dynamics of the patient-therapist relationship and the right-brain to right-brain socioaffective attunement which takes place (Schore, 2003, p. 80). Psychotherapy may be viewed as a process of exploring a patient's affective states with an intention to transmute and reorganise their regulatory structures. 'This is a dyadic venture in which the therapist serves an affect regulating self-object function' (Schore, 1994, p. 449). Schore comments, 'The psychotherapist's establishment of a dyadic affective "growth promoting environment" influences the ontogeny of homeostatic, self-regulatory systems' (Schore, 1994, p. 463). Psychotherapy may also play a role in fostering neuroplasticity; Cozolino draws the following conclusion:

> The power of psychotherapy to change the brain rests in its ability to recognize and alter unintegrated or dysregulated neural networks. As psychotherapy has progressed through the last century, the need for a balance between an empathic relationship and an exposure to manageable stress has been a repeated theme. In this interpersonal and emotional context, the use of language based learning in the form of co-constructed narratives, psychoeducation, and reality testing have also proven central to successful treatment. As knowledge of neural plasticity and neurogenesis increases, so will our ability to impact and alter the brain. The possibility exists that sensitive periods can be reinstated in the context of psychotherapy, and that stress can be utilized in a controlled manner to "reedit" emotional memories (Cozolino, 2002, p. 302).

Neuro linguistic programming employs language to both elicit the unconscious deep structures which form a client's narrative of experience, and also, to assist in the reorganization of internal structures and neuro-associative conditioning. For the initial module on the MSc in Psycho-Social Studies course, I undertook an investigation into the neuroscientific basis of neuro linguistic programming. This formative study showed that this methodology yields more fruitful results when the applied technique is accompanied with an affective charge (Rowan, 2009a, p. 14). Empathy is maintained with the use of patterns of hypnotic language established by Milton Erickson, and sometimes referred to as, 'the art of being artfully vague' (Harrison, 2001, p. 45).

In this paper it has been shown that experiences of numinosity encourage neurogenesis (Rossi, 2002, p.12). Schore confirms that allowing feelings of uncertainty to emerge may also induce a sense of wonder and encourage a client to explore. He remarks, 'a dynamic systems theory perspective of the psychotherapy process holds that both the therapist and the patient need to understand that destabilization and the tolerance of uncertainty may be fundamental to a healthy process, and that such experiences are important opportunities for change' (Schore, 2003, p. 95).

Orsucci reports, studies reveal that neuroplasticity is fostered by meditative and mindfulness states. Cortical thickness in brain regions associated with attention, interoception and sensory processing were thicker in meditation participants than matched controls, including the prefrontal cortex and anterior insula. He writes, 'Between-group differences in prefrontal cortical thickness were most pronounced in older participants, suggesting that meditation might offset age-related cortical thinning' (Orsucci, 2009, p. 25). In *Hidden Depths,* Waterfield recounts experiments in which the brain activity of subjects placed in an altered state of consciousness, commonly known as a hypnotic trance, was shown to be different to both their normal patterns of brain activity and those of a control group who were also receiving and following the same motor and eye-movement instructions. He comments:

> If there is such a thing as the hypnotic trance, what kind of a state is it? Milton Erickson's definition, penned for the 1954 Encyclopaedia Britannica, seems admirable. It is:

162

A special psychological state with certain
physiological attributes resembling sleep
only superficially, and characterized by a
functioning of the individual at a level of
awareness other than the ordinary state,
a level of awareness termed, for
convenience in conceptualization,
unconscious or subconscious awareness.
(Waterfield, 2002, p.39).

In neuro linguistic programming, the hypnotic trance is utilised to create
an environment in which neurogenesis can be stimulated and new
pathways of experience opened for the individual. In this sense the
hypnotic trance is an internal environment for change which is nested
within the external transformational environment of the consulting room,
which itself may become neuro-associated with sensory experiences such
as relaxation, along with representing a safe haven for exploring
resolution of historical difficulties and the genesis of transformation.

Schore describes this very same process in a psychotherapeutic context:

Because the holding environment is organized by
preverbal communications the continuously
attuned clinician must initiate a right brain
regulatory strategy that allows him/her to
remain in a: state of "regressive openness and
receptivity." The essential step in a creating
holding environment in which an affect-
communicating reconnection can be forged is
the therapist's ability, initially at a nonverbal level,
to detect, recognise, monitor, and autoregulate
the countertransferential stressful alterations in
his/her bodily state that are evoked by the
patient's transferential communications. Thus,
the clinician simultaneously monitors the
information coming from the patient as well as

his/her own psychobiological response to this emotional communication (Schore, 2003, p.95).

Sasportas notes that our experiences of relating with our first container, our mother, may be reflected in the manner in which we subsequently relate with the larger container of society (Sasportas, 1985, p. 331). The environments in which we are situated may each perform a role of containment, acting as crucibles within which ontogenetic development may occur. In *Attachment, Intimacy and Autonomy*, Holmes reports that holding and containment are central functions of supportive therapy and can be understood developmentally as, '... concentric circles of attachment' (Holmes, 1996, p. 129). The consulting room provides just such a crucible, enabling an individual to explore and resolve issues in an environment in which neuro-associated affects may be experienced and reorganized into new pathways of experience. Fostering a secure base benefits the society in which a person is situated, as well as the individual undergoing therapy.

Throughout the life span, attachment systems may be activated by threats to security. A variety of things may represent a secure base for an individual, the most obvious being a parent or a romantic partner. In addition to therapists, other care workers such as hospital staff can become surrogate attachment figures and non-clinical adults have been known to describe their secure base as pets, family, close friends, hot baths, duvets, photograph albums, being in touch with nature, favourite books and music (Holmes, 2001, p 29). Kirkpatrick reports from his research into the psychology of religions that it is not only religious figures and leaders, but also God who may become a secure base (Kirkpatrick, 2005, p.65). Mental health bodies advise, 'a stable routine and structure at home will provide a secure base for your child', (Collingwood, 2009), implying that anticipatory time-bound structures may also signify security for an individual.

Contemporary attachment theorists such as Ainsworth and Main have placed an emphasis not on the typology of attachment behaviour but on the degree of coherence, or incoherence in the subject's account of childhood memories (Mitchell, 2000, p.85). In the *Search for a Secure Base*, Holmes suggests that autobiographical competence; the ability to describe one's past, however painful, clearly and coherently without denial or being overwhelmed, is a manifestation of secure attachment and reflexive function (Holmes, 2001, p. 105).

At this stage of the investigation it may be concluded that the environment interacts with innate gene potentials, allowing certain combinations of neural networks and affects to project the ontological and embodied psychology in a determinate trajectory. The subsequent orientation of attachment behaviours and regulation of affects can be re-directed by further interactions throughout the lifespan and it is possible to construct a therapeutic environment of care with the deliberate purpose of fostering change, inducing neurgenesis and a reorganization of affect regulation and attachment responses. The study will now address the topic of agency to explore the question of the self and volition in affective neuroscience.

<u>Agency: the sense of self and the free will of volition in affective neuroscience:</u>

Recent advances in brain scanning and imaging technologies suggest that the sense of agency we call 'the self' cannot be localized in a single defined area of the brain and appears to emerge as a function of multiple systems of implicit and explicit memory (Cozolino, 2006, p. 338). However, some neuroscientists disagree with this position, claiming it to be overly materialistic. Experiments are conducted in a quest to identify a spiritual sense of agency; what Pinker describes as, 'the ghost in the machine' (Pinker, 2002, p.9). In *The Spiritual Brain*, Beauregard and O'Leary report on a variety of experiments conducted in the quest to find a God-gene or God-neuron (Beauregard and O'Leary, 2007, p. 42). They argue against the materialistic view, suggesting that mind and brain are separate and that just because neuroscientists have not found a neural referent for God, it does not mean that there is not one. They propose that religious and spiritual experiences arise from an encounter with an independent spiritual force (Beauregard and O'Leary, 2007, p. 292). In the chapter entitled, 'Does the God Module even exist?', a discussion is undertaken of the role of the temporal lobe in imbibing experience with a sense of joy and harmony during spiritual experience. It is argued that the suggestion that temporal-lobe epilepsy forming the basis of spiritual experience is an epistemological error, brought about by the atheist agendas in materialistic neuroscientists and that, 'although the temporal lobes appear to be implicated in the perception of contacting a spiritual reality, as they are in many other types of perception, they are not a "God spot" or "God module" (Beauregard and O'Leary, 2007, p. 76). Trimble agrees that epilepsy is associated with religious ecstasy and with religiosity in some patients, though such expressions often lack the musicality and prosody of poetry; a pattern which is identical to the expressions recorded in the past of many religious prophets and may be found in other neuropsychiatric illness such as bipolar affective disorder or schizophrenia. "Religious fever" does not point to a sense of agency (Trimble, 2007, P. 158). However, creative expressions of the self through artistic mediums such as poetry correlate with right-brain affective experience and an allegorical, symbolic and pre-conscious language (Trimble, 2007, p. 186).

The emergence of the self appears to be constructed from many layers of neural processing and ontological development (Cozolino, 2006, p. 338). Capra asserts that cognition is an emergent function of autopietic networks; a process, rather than an object (Capra, 1996, p. 259). Recent studies show that single neurons, while functioning as part of a network, hold an individual capacity for problem solving within their environment and emit discrete audio signals at around 40 hertz, in which they appear to address one another (Ford, 2010, p. 27). Panksepp comments, 'it has become fashionable to question the existence of central agencies within the brain that permit conscious awareness. Many claim there is no coherent neural referent for the pronoun "I" (Panksepp, 2005, p. 311).

Consciousness does not appear to arise from any single region or neural network of the brain, but seems to be an emergent function which arises from the integration and synchrony of cycles of neural processing (Cozolino, 2002, p153). In *The Feeling of What Happens*, Domasio describes the emergence of narrative as a process which begins with a proto-conscious core self:

> ...neural patterns which become images, images being the same fundamental currency in which the description of the consciousness-causing object is also carried out. Most importantly, the images that constitute this narrative are incorporated in the stream of thoughts. The images in the consciousness narrative flow like shadows along with the images of the object for which they are providing an unwitting, unsolicited comment. To come back to the metaphor of movie-in-the-brain, they are *within* the movie. There is no external spectator (Domasio, 1999, p171).

Domasio asserts the autobiographical self is constituted by implicit memories of multiple instances of past experiences which grow continuously and may be partly remodelled to reflect new experiences. Sets of memories which describe identity and person can be reactivated as a neural pattern and made explicit as images (Domasio, 1999, p.174). Edelman and Tononi confer, describing the formation of the autobiographical self as, 'the remembered present'; a higher-order of consciousness which can place itself in a scheme of the past, present and anticipated future, which, in its most developed form has a semantic and linguistic capability (Edelman and Tononi, 2000, p. 103). Spence comments on the implications this has for the experience of free will, or volition. Subjective awareness arises only after a train of neural activity has been set in motion. In addition, we orient temporally towards an anticipated future of possibilities. He comments, 'We seem to be a most curious breed of dysfunctional clairvoyants, looking forward to the theoretically possible while only becoming aware of what we have embarked upon (our verdical physical acts) once they have already started' (Spence, 2009, p. 125).

In the field of consciousness studies, the understanding of how matter becomes subjective experience is referred to as 'the hard problem of consciousness' (Chalmers, 2008, p. 226). One model for understanding the subjective awareness of experience is the concept of qualia. In *Language, Consciousness and Culture*, Jackendoff defines qualia as, 'The term of art for the form in which consciousness presents itself is qualia'. (Jackendoff, 2007, p.79). Qualia refers to specific qualities of subjective experience, such as: loudness, warmth and colour. Qualia are derived from a primary sensation, corresponding to unique states in the dynamic core. Tononi and Edelman report that these states are, '...differentiated from billions of other states within a neural space comprising a large number of dimensions. The relevant dimensions are given by the number of neuronal groups whose activities, integrated through reentrant interactions, constitute a dynamic core of high complexity. Qualia are therefore high-dimensional discriminations' (Edelman and Tononi, p. 175).

The topography of language may be viewed as phonological, syntactic and semantic or conceptual in structure (Jackendoff, 2007, p.81). In *The Neuroscience of Psychotherapy*, Cozolino describes the networks of the semantic aspects of language explicitly:

> Although the semantic aspects of language are usually lateralized to the left hemisphere, the right contributes the emotional and prosodic element of speech. The left-hemisphere language network relies on the convergence of auditory, visual, and sensory

information from the temporal, occipital, and parietal lobes, respectively. Wernicke's area in the temporal lobe receives input from the primary auditory area, and organizes it into meaningful bits of information. The convergence zone connects sounds, sights, and touch so that cross-modal connections can be made, allowing us to name things we touch and hear without visual cues (Cozolino, 2002, p. 112).

These sophisticated networks are also called into play when a memory is recalled;

It is also necessary for the development of sign language, where words take the form of gestures. This sophisticated and highly processed information projects forward to Broca's area, where expressive speech is organized. Nerve fibres linking language areas to the rest of the frontal lobes allow both spoken and internal language to guide behaviour and regulate affect. The integrative properties of language may be unequalled by any other function of the brain. Creating and recalling a story requires the convergence of multisensory emotional, temporal, and memory capabilities that bridge all vectors of neural networks. In this way, language organizes the brain and can be used to reorganize it in psychotherapy (Cozolino, 2002, p. 113).

Qualia are discriminated through an experiential filter that reflects an individual's history of being (Edelman and Tononi, p. 175), while meaning and belief play interlocking and complementary roles in the interpretation of speech. This relationship is strengthened by emphasizing the connection between our grounds for attributing beliefs to speakers, and our grounds for assigning meanings to their utterances (Davidson, 1974, cited in Martinich, 2001, p.464). If the function of language is the expression and communication of thoughts, then semantics may be thought of as the organization of thoughts that language can express; a conceptual structure (Jackendoff, 2004, p. 123). Cozolino asserts that, 'The existence of a conscious self most likely depends on language' (Cozolino, 2002, p. 156). The relationship between experience and subjective awareness may be viewed in terms of percepts and concepts. Jackendoff comments:

> The structures that a linguist writes on the page, say syntactic trees, are intended as representations of what is in the mind. However, I would maintain that what is in the mind is best not thought of as a representation or a symbol of anything. The reason is that the words "representation" and "symbol" imply an interpreter or perceiver: it is not just that *this* represents or symbolizes *that,* but implicitly that *this* represents or symbolizes *that* **to so-and-so.** But a person in whose mind syntactic structures reside does not perceive them; rather, the person perceives a linguistic utterance by virtue of having these structures in his or her mind. The only thing that "perceives" syntactic structures is the faculties of mind that process and store syntactic structures, and in fact the term "perceive" is itself suspect in this context (Jankendoff, 2007, p. 5).

The relationship between the anatomy of the brain and conscious awareness holds one key to understanding the structural dynamics of the self as an autonomous agent. Neuroscience continues to refine its comprehension of experience as technology develops. At this time or writing, a technology has not yet emerged which can identify the neural referent for the self. On the one hand, the current uncertainty may be viewed as a problem for the field of neuroscience, providing a battle ground upon which materialists and vitalists compete for supremacy (Capra, 1996, p. 24). However, this very same uncertainty affords the opportunity for imaginative hypothesis and interpretation of data in the philosophy of affective neuroscience. For example, Panksepp comments that, contrary to the current trend, he would advocate the position that a central processor does exist (Panksepp, 2005, p.311). Jackendoff contributes the following to the debate;

> If we are to take seriously the relation between mind and brain, this is the only possible view of mental structures. The neurons deep inside the brain that are responsible for cognition have no privileged access to the "real world"; they interact only with other neurons. Contact with the "real world" is established only through long chains of connection leading eventually to sensory and motor neurons. If this is the hardware on which mental capacities "run," then mental capacities too are necessarily limited in their contact with the "real world." They are sensitive to the outside environment only insofar as they are connected through functional (or computational) links to the sensory and motor capacities (Jankendoff, 2007, p. 5).

However, Panksepp is explicit that he does not view the self as an internal self-observer; '... an infinite regress of sensory homunculi observing each other ad infinitum' (Panksepp, 2005, p. 311). Rather he postulates the existence of a primitive motor-action homunculus which is akin to a primal representation of a self, residing in the core primary consciousness (Panksepp, 2005, p. 311). Koch agrees and not only supports the proposition of the existence of a non-conscious homunculus, but also proposes a description of its neural mechanism. He argues that qualia are symbols; a particular property of highly paralleled feedback networks which carry an enormous amount of explicit and implicit information. The information is expressed by the neural correlates of consciousness at the essential nodes, while the implicit information is distributed across a large population of neurons which make up the neural correlate's penumbra. He comments:

> A bright red light triggers a simple color quale, while looking at a dog or a face leads to a much richer and detailed percept. All three arise rapidly and can disappear equally quickly. Conversely, the quale associated with the feeling of *deja vu* or being angry

172

takes a lot longer to develop and subside and may have fewer associations. As a class, the phenomenal feelings associated with imagination and memory tend to be less vivid than those generated by an external stimulus, although people's ability to conjure up mental images varies considerably. The associated qualia are much weaker, less intense, and less lifelike, with fewer details. I believe that the degree of vividness manifests itself at the neuronal level as the extent of the coalition representing the neural correlates of consciousness. The more widespread the neuronal membership of the winning coalition, the more details and aspects are consciously expressed and the more vivid the percept (Koch, 2004, 301).

The difference in vividness between a percept and concept can be likened to the experience of seeing a red tomato and then later recalling the image of the tomato. When a tomato is seen, a higher number of neurons in the visual cortex are fired than are those which are represented in the prefrontal cortex. This coalition of fired neurons are relayed downward into the premotor cortex and up again to the prefrontal cortex and on to the relevant motor structures (Crick and Koch, 2008, p. 568). In this sense, one might say that a percept image that we are observing has a high number of visual pixels while a conceptual memory of something which we had already seen, has fewer pixels; thus, we are able to discern the difference between something we can observe in the external physical world and an internally constructed illusion. When neural coalitions are active above a certain threshold, the unconscious activity emerges into conscious awareness. Different networks may be stimulated simultaneously, allowing for attention and binding of phenomena to occur; attention and consciousness are separate processes. 'Attention can be usefully divided into rapid, saliency-driven, bottom-up forms, and slower, volitionally controlled, top-down forms (Crick and Koch, 2008, p. 573).
It is beyond the scope of this paper to rigorously survey the topic of volition. However, it would be pertinent to the study to bring a small number of points into the investigation. One of the founders of neuro linguistic programming, Richard Bandler, proposed a metaphor for self control in the book, *Using Your Brain For A Change*, stating that rather than being like a passenger in a runaway bus, it is better to gain control and drive it oneself (Bandler, 1985, p. 8). In *The Neuroscience of*

Psychotherapy, Cozolino suggests that self control is an illusion, remarking, 'Although we feel convinced we are driving, actually, we may be dozing on the back seat merely dreaming that we are driving' (Cozolino, 2002, p. 158). In 1983 Benjamin Libet conducted a series of experiments which revealed that neural stimulus occurs prior to conscious awareness and is mediated by a sense of self which has a veto-response option, able to halt any undesired action from proceeding (Banks and Pocket, 2008, p. 657). This veto-mechanism, which Spence refers to as 'free-won't' (Spence, 2009, p. 147), may be interpreted as a non-physical nonderterministic agent for which there is no neural antecedent (Banks and Pocket, 2008, p. 667). Conversely, it may be viewed as a result of the dysregulated affect of what is known as 'shame' (Schore, 1994, p. 240).

As remarked in the introduction of this paper, the question of causality has been a focus of attention in philosophy since ancient Greece (Dennet, 1984, p. 1), and a contemporary systems approach may offer a revision of the fate versus free-will dualism. In *The Actor's Brain*, Spence concludes that a volitional response does exist and is bounded by multiple physical, psychological and social constraints. These include; a social agentic environment, the physical environment, body and brain anatomy, neurochemistry, physiology, psychology and cognitive executive function, the phenomenology of temporal positioning, attention and mirror systems, or capacity for empathy, and genetics (Spence, 2009, p. 364). In other words, volition has a structural form which is one of a pattern situated within a relational environment; this is akin to relational-structure of the sense of self, the architecture of the brain's neural networking and of each individual cell.

This suggests that the environment itself appears to form an element of agency. Spence attests that we are social beings, formed as a consequence of what others do for us, 'We exist at the interface of nature and nurture' (Spence, 2009, p. 395). A conclusion that may be drawn from the findings of this survey suggests that not only is our sense of agency formed from the self-generating trajectory of our personal history and epigenetic potentials, but we are also ontologically temporally positioned with the orientation of our anticipated future.

The context within which working memory and autobiographical narrative are situated appears to play a substantial role in determining which of our innate potentials will be salient and will either facilitate a regeneration of the self and circumstances or prompt a bifurcation on to new pathways of experience. In *The Master and His Emissary*, McGilchrist reports that the concern of the brain's left hemisphere is one of being explicitly fixed with what is known, while the right hemisphere experience is implicit, exploratory and evolving (McGilchrist, 2009, p. 174), suggesting that the brain is architecturally configured to hold the potentials for both determinism and agency and it is our environment which plays a key role drawing the appropriate and adaptive potentials into salient operation.

Reflections on the study: a review of how the findings of the study relate
to previous psycho-social research:

Pinker's remark that it there is a general confusion between explanation
and exculpation (Pinker, 2002, p. 179), addresses the important issue of
the nature of morality and responsibility. If the sense of agency or self is
an illusion of consciousness, what prompts the genesis and maintenance
of morality? Dennet atests that morality is an emergent function of
society (Dennet, 1984, p. 158), which suggests moral codes play a role in
the autopiesis of social networks. Score reports that the experience of an
emotion often called 'shame', plays a role in both the development of the
socialising process and affective self-regulation (Schore, 1994, p. 199). In
The Civilizing Process, Elias concurs that social constraint brings about self-
constraint (Elias, 2000, p. 367). Conclusions drawn in a previous
psychosocial research found that both social networks and the landscape
which contains society can become a secure base for an individual, In
addition, the study concluded, 'The relationship between landscape and
identity may be both introjective and intrajective; each impressing itself
upon the other' (Rowan, 2009b, p. 33). This broadens the view of Spence
that the environment has the capacity to be socio-agentic (Spence, 2009,
p. 364), suggesting that the autopietic container in which the permeable
self and society are situated may also hold an agentic quality for the
individual.

In two case studies previously presented in a paper researching
attachment theory, the role of the dyadic relationship, experiences in the
early home environment and familial memetic discourses (Blackmore,
1999, p. 99) in forming affect regulation and attachment responses was
established. It was suggested that these continue to function throughout
the lifespan (Rowan, 2009c, p. 8). However, the findings of this study
regarding determinism and the capacity for inducing change, whether by
the hand of one's own agency or in a dyaditic therapeutic environment,
suggests a review of the two case studies may yield a new illumination.
The review will begin with a brief recapitulation of each subject.

Recapitulation:

With regard to the presentation of the previous study, each subject was given a pseudonym in order to protect their identity, and for continuity, the same names will be used once again: Dylan and Amber.

Dylan:

Dylan is a white single male in his mid-forties; a divorcee with no children. He lives alone in a house he owns, situated in a rural village in close proximity to both his place of work and the family home. He has had just one partner and much of his life appears to revolve around his family. He reports that he was previously, in the opinion of his family, an overly boisterous child and this behaviour was nurtured out of him. Although he has not revealed the details of the process, he agrees that he became subdued by a fear of disapproval.

As an adult, Dylan lives as if his affect is permanently over regulated and controlled by shame. His choice of car is influenced by familial needs and wishes; the weekly routine is constant, with Sunday lunch being an event unchanged since his childhood. There is certainly a lack of exploration in his life and he stoically strives to manage on a continuum of maintaining sameness. To an observer, his apethia may seem to be apathy. He has maintained the same blue collar job for twenty five years with no ambitious thought for promotion. He reports that a small number of failed attempts to explore new adventures in life have left their mark and as a result he is resigned to what he regards as his place in life. When asked if he believed in fate he gave an unequivocal, 'yes', agreeing that his past had undoubtedly shaped and determined both his present and his future.

Dylan demonstrates obsessive compulsive disorder behaviours, which remain without formal diagnosis or therapeutic treatment. He reports that he has never experienced therapy and has no wish to, almost referring to it as something to avoid. With gentle questioning he revealed he believes he has a lot of repressed anger which would be extremely difficult to confront. Instead, he is constantly challenged to maintain his status quo, resisting change whenever he can. In addition to learning to be afraid of his parent's disapproval, he was bullied at school, and this experience was repeated in his only adult relationship. An incident of rejection at the age of seventeen is a salient feature of his narrative and supports his present orientation of giving more value to avoiding the risks of rejection than forming affectional bonds with an adult and his own offspring. He reports that he is concerned about expression of his temper, preferring to maintain consistently passive. He appears to self consciously attend to regulating his affect in the company of others. We have discussed his choice to avoid rejection and subsequently evade fatherhood, and it is with this emotive topic that a dissonance is observable (Cooper, 2007, p. 68).

The previous study concluded that, on the surface, it would appear that Dylan has an avoidant attachment style. When recounting his past, he adopts the position of the defended subject and maintains a subdued affect; normalising his history and is seemingly uninterested in any form of therapeutic resolution of historical issues which continue to cause him either distress or influence current life experience (Hollway & Jefferson, 2000, p 19). Dylan is hesitant to begin talking, but once underway, he expresses himself with an easy disposition and good humour. On the surface he is a paradox; a secure man with no attachments. Ontologically, it would appear that Dylan is somehow stuck in a pattern of allowing the structure of developmental chapters of his life to be determined by the trajectory of his past.

However, beneath the surface, a different picture emerges; maintenance of distance, controlled affect and disinterest in actively resolving issues and bringing positive change into his life confirm that Dylan has an avoidant attachment style which is beginning to show subtle signs of bifurcation. Recent conversations suggest that Dylan's desire to avoid conflict means he also avoids stepping into the life he would like to live, and the pressure of holding himself in is proving too great. Since his participation in the research he has purchased a car of his own choosing, though certain elements of the purchase were still directed by parental guidance, and has formulated strategies for developing a social life. He desires to actively seek relationships and although he has not proved successful to date, it is possible he will find new pathways in life.

Amber:

Amber is a British-Asian woman, married and now in her early forties. She is a career professional, a carer for her disabled husband and has no children.

Amber has a lifestyle which sits in complete contrast to Dylan. At the age of thirty, she embarked on a therapeutic journey that has taken a variety of forms. When asked if she believed in fate, she stated, 'The Only thing that is fated is death'. She holds the view that it is possible to change and actively pursues transformation.

She does agree with Dylan on one point; that the trajectory of life is set into play by one's history and experiences in the early home environment. Amber's history is one of severe, regular and systematic sexual abuse from more than one family member. This began when she was four years old and did not cease until she reached adulthood. The perpetrators were her brothers and she was also abused by a religious leader while in a Mosque. She reported that, to her, abuse to females in her environment from males seemed ubiquitous, however, did this not include her father, who constituted a secure base. Amber was fostered at birth for three months and, she reports, formed an affectionate bond with her foster parents. There was degree of affection found here which was absent in her relationship with her mother, who seemed detached and cold; preoccupied with her own concerns and that of maintaining the reputation of the family name within their culture. Cozolino reports that the disorganized attachment which results from separation distress can be introjected from a mother who also suffers from unresolved trauma (Cozolino, 2006, p. 231).

Amber's communication style is generally clear and concise, which occasionally changes as strong affects arise and then subside. I mirror her style when interviewing and I am conscious of my position as a defended researcher, aware that I am regulating my own affect with deliberate and gentle patience (Gilmour, 2009, p.125). In the research interviews, affects emerged during a discussion on Amber's choice to abstain from entering motherhood. During these interviews, she attested that this was almost a choice by proxy, and it was a decision made by her husband which removed her ability to be free to choose to be a mother or not. Recent

181

conversations with Amber have revealed she has a new perspective on this issue, and the findings of the study show how this has arisen. Since the research interviews, Amber has undergone intense training in Buddhism which has illuminated new perceptions of both herself and of the path in life she wishes to take. The numinous experiences of meditation have enabled her to draw to the surface deeper memories of the genesis of the abuse and this has also afforded the opportunity to re-organise the narrative in which she holds her history.

However, the path of recovery is often long and arduous and Amber's affects can display dysregulation depending on the context of the environment she is in. During a recent conversation I asked her if she believed that undertaking any aspect of her therapeutic journey; whether counselling, neuro linguistic programming or indeed the sanctuary of a meditative Buddhist retreat had brought about an enduring change, or changes in her life. She confirmed that it had, but when asked to name at least one example, displayed a dissonant amnesia. Three days later, during a support phone call on the first day of her next retreat, she enthused that not only has she accomplished many enduring changes, but she could list them; which she duly did. Within two days of returning home, one of the behaviours with which she had reported an enduring change resurfaced. This suggests that Amber's orientation is state dependant and contextualised with the environment in which she is either currently operating, or of which she retains sense of an emotional presence (Rossi 1993, p.80). She often speaks of events in life as a 'break-state'.

However, Amber is certainly mounting every campaign possible to transform her life and leave the shadows of the past behind. During the interview process of the research, her voice significantly changed, presenting a new resonance and on recognising this I formed the conclusion that she is learning to establish an internal secure base.

Amber now reports that although her current lifestyle and circumstance are very different from the dreams she had in her twenties about her future, rather than being angry or frustrated with life, she is now experiencing a sense of inner security and self acceptance. She remains highly ambitious while still concerned about material prospects and intimate relationships, but these concerns now rest upon an emerging sense of peace; the product of purposefully seeking to outgrow the past and develop an internal secure base.

Reflexive note:

During the course of the study I have experienced a number of reflexive revisions of my own relationship with the material. The sensitive period of reorganisation of neural networks during puberty, coincided with what I believe to be one of my first actions in countering the predisposition of my life in the autistic spectrum. This study shows that I had intuitively begun the process of learning to relate during a critical neural growth period. Subsequently, I became a self taught musician during my teens and early twenties, and training in hypnotherapy during my thirties has increased my experiences of numinosity, which I now understand to be more beneficial than I had previously realised. I have developed coping mechanisms to the extent that people with whom I have superficial contact are often completely unaware that I experience life through the lens of the autistic spectrum.

However, upon closer inspection, facets of my Asperger's and dyspraxic nature are easily observed. For example, the research material on volition brought my dyspraxia into clearer focus, though I am still not entirely sure what guides my hand to peel my thumb instead of the potato I can clearly see myself holding. The physical side of life remains the most difficult in which to apply therapeutic techniques. Another area which remains unadaptive, and yet brings a sense of comfort, is that of literalism. I described this dynamic in the last of the preliminary papers for the MSc (Rowan, 2003d, p. 6), and I now understand that I have taken a stoic approach towards this issue. Rather than attempt to modify or change my tendency to literalism, I have instead utilised this fated pre-disposition to pedantry as a skill in both writing and my therapeutic work, transforming the nature of my experience by practicing a purposeful apethia.

Before concluding the paper, I shall first bring this reflexive note to a close with a sample transcript taken from my final tutorial concerned with this paper, which took place two days before this study's completion.

The identifying initials are: D, for David Rowan and T, for tutor.

D: I mentioned in an email, that before embarking on it, I wrote a mini article on my 'before position', so I could compare it with an 'after' to see if it's caused any change.

T: Yes.

D: And the before position was, I've always had this, an intuitive sense that somehow nature and nurture work adjacent with each other, that they are not exclusive.

T: Hmmm ...

D: And that we're creatures of both. Um, what I found through doing the research is that time is a very important thing, so 'when you are', but also how agentic the environment is. And how much these things, that there isn't necessarily a self, we haven't necessarily got an agency, as far as we can tell, but these things seem to coalesce together to produce a sense of agency. I didn't realise, oddly enough for an astrologer, I didn't realise how important the environment was, in shaping, moulding, containing and producing content. I've always thought of myself as a being, situated in; so I am a me, and I can be influenced by the environment, um, but I never would have thought that, so strongly, the environment plays a role in shaping what I am. That's a new realisation a dawning awareness of ...

T: And indeed, given that you're recording this, this is a sort of back-to-front psycho-social interview; you could literally transcript what you've just said. I'm saying that because, um, actually, what you've just done is to combine autobiographical references with a description of something you did, to help you do this writing. And your, spoken word, is different to your written word. You speak more rhythmically and simply than you write; it is a different cadence and different rhythm.

I find, as the end of the study draws near, that a new voice has appeared in the landscape of my understanding of life as a direct result of undertaking this study, suggesting that the inner landscape of our reality is not merely held by the environment, nor is it a passive recipient of its influence. Rather, the emergent hypothesis shows that the local environment, nested within concentric patterns of ever more distant environments, appears to be one of four key elements of what constitutes the self in the present moment. Both the physical and socioaffective environments are structurally coupled with our genotype, personal-history and the temporal position in our ontology, forming the agentic structure and pattern of who we are and who we may become.

Conclusion:

This study has shown that we are an autopietic system, comprised of millions of other autopietic systems at a micro-biological level, situated within an autopietic socio-affective environment, which itself is nested within a culture, a society and wider eco-environment. Epigenetic systems of embodied potential are influenced by environmental interactions which foster the specific experiential qualities of a stepwise ontologenetic development. Socioaffective right-brain experiences sculpt the brain and give shape to the neural and synaptic networks which host the emergent affective and cognitive processing. Narratives of beliefs and introjected memetic discourses enmesh with attachment behaviours which are adaptive and undergo periods of reorganization in response to the environment and experiences which carry an affective charge throughout the entire lifespan. Adaptive neurogenesis can be deliberately induced in therapeutic care-giving relationships and activities which induce numinosity. It appears that the self is an emergent function of process and is both hardwired and softwired to maintain and yet evolve the system as a living organism. It has the free will to select from a wide set of choices, the parameters of which are nonetheless pre-determined by the path of its personal history and current ontological and socio-environmental context.

While the scope of this paper does not allow for a more thorough investigation of determinism and agency in affective neuroscience, it has consolidated trains of thought regarding the nature and nurture debate and has opened new pathways towards viewing the role of the environment in the landscape of human experience. There is most certainly a case for further research and development in this area, and it is my intention to use the findings gained from the research outlined in this paper as a platform upon which to conduct further study and investigation.

Bibliography:

Bandler, R., 1985, *Using Your Brain For A Change*, Real People Press.
Banks W., P, Pockett, S., 2008, *The Blackwell Companion To Consciousness: Benjamin Libet's Work on the Neuroscience of Free Will*, Blackwell Publishing.
Barrett, L., Dunbar, R., Lycett, J., 2002, *human evolutionary psychology*, Palgrave.
Bateman, A., and Holmes, J., 1995, *Introduction to Psychoanalysis*, Routledge.
Beauregard, M., O'Leary, D., 2007, *The Spiritual Brain: A Neuroscientist's Case For The Existence Of The Soul*, Harper One.
Blackmore, S., 1999, *The Meme Machine*, Oxford University Press.
Bowlby, J., 1979, *The Making and Breaking of Affectional Bonds*, Routeledge.
Bowlby, J., 1988, *A Secure Base*, Routeledge.
Campion, N., 2008, *The Dawn of Astrology: A cultural History of Western Astrology; The Ancient and Classical Worlds*, Continuum.
Capra, F., 1996, *The Web of Life*, Harper Collins.
Clarke, L., 2009, *Middle-class children have better genes, says former schools chief... and we just have to accept it*, The Daily Mail, http://www.dailymail.co.uk/news/article-1180701/Middle-class-children-better-genes-says-schools-chief--just-accept-it.html, sourced March 2010.
Chalmers, D., 2008, *The Blackwell Companion To Consciousness: The Hard Problem of Consciousness*, Blackwell Publishing.
Collingwood, J., *Helping a Family Member with a Mental Disorder*, http://psychcentral.com/lib/2006/helping-a-family-member-with-a-mental-disorder/
Cooper, J., 2007, *Cognitive Dissonance*, Sage.
Corrigall, J., and Wilkinson, H., 2003, *Revolutionary Connections*, H. Karnac Books Ltd
Cozolino, L., 2002, *The Neuroscience of Psychotherapy: Building And Rebuilding The Human Brain*, W.W. Norton and Company Inc.
Cozolino, L., 2006, *The Neuroscience of Human Relationships: Attachment and the Developing Social Brain*, W.W. Norton and Company Inc.
Crick, F., and Koch, C., 2008, *The Blackwell Companion To Consciousness: A neurobiological framework of consciousness*, Blackwell Publishing.
Curry, P., 1992, *A Confusion Of Prophets: Victorian And Edwardian Astrology*, Collins and Brown.

Davidson, D., 1974, *Belief and the Basis of Meaning*, cited in Martininch, A. P., *ed*, (2001), *The Philosophy of Language*. Oxford: Oxford university Press.

Dawkins, R., 2006 edition, *The Sefish Gene*, Oxford University Press.

Dennet, D., 1984, *Elbow Room: The Varieties Of Free Will Worth Wanting*, Oxford University Press.

Domasio, A., 1995, *Descarte's Error: Emotion, Reason and the Human Brain*, Harper Perennial

Domasio, A., 1999, *The Feeling of What Happens: Body, Emotion And The Making Of Consciousness*, William Heinemann: London.

Dowling, J. E., 2004, *The Great Brain Debate: Nature Or Nurture ?*, Joseph Henry Press.

Edelman, G. M., and Tononi, G., 2000, *Consciousness: How Matter Becomes Imagination*, Penguin Books Ltd.

Elias, N., 2000, *The Civilizing Process*, Blackwell Publishing.

Fairclough, N., 1992, *Discourse and Social Change*, Polity.

Folensbee, R. W., 2007, The Neuroscience of Psychological Therapies, Cambridge University Press.

Fonagy, P., Gergely G., Hurist, E., Target, M., 2004, *Affect Regulation, Mentalization, and the Development of the Self*, other Press.

Ford, B. J., 2010, *The secret power of the single cell*, New Scientist magazine No2757.

Geert, P. V., 2009, *Chaos and Complexity in Psychology: The Theory of Nonlinear Dynamical Systems: Non Linear Dynamical Systems in Developmental Psychology*, Cambridge University Press.

Gilmore, R., 2009, *Fear-And Psycho-Social Interviewing: Researching Beneath The Surface*, Karnac.

Glaser, D., 2003, *Revolutionary Connections: Psychotherapy and Neuroscience: Early experience, attachment and the brain*, Karnac.

Harrison, M., *The Master Practitioner Suite Volumes One, Two and Three*, 2001, Tao Te Publishing.

Hinshelwood, R. D., 1989, *A dictionary of Kleinian thought*, Free Association Press.

Holloway, W. Jefferson, T., 2000, *Doing Qualitive Research Differently*, Sage.

Holmes, J., 1996, *Attachment, Intimacy and Autonomy*, Jason Aronson Inc.

Holmes, J., 2001, *The Search for the Secure Base: Attachment Theory and Psychotherapy*, Routledge.

Jackendoff, R., 2004, *Foundations of Language*, Oxford University Press.
Jackendoff, R., 2007, *Language, Consciousness, Culture: Essays on Mental Structure*, The MIT Press.
Koch, C., *The Quest for Consciousness: A Neurobiological Approach*, 2004, Roberts &b Company Publishers.
Kirkpatrick, L. A., 2005, *Attachment, Evolution, And The Psychology of Religion*, The Guildford Press.
Laland, K. N., Brown, G., 2002, *Sense & Nonsense: evolutionary perspectives on human behaviour*, Oxford University Press.

Laplanche, J., and Pontalis, J-B., 1973, *The Language of Psychoanalysis*, W.W. Norton and Company.

Lipton, B. H., 2005, *The Biology Of Belief*, Hay House Inc.
Lloyd, D., Rossi, E. L., 1992, *Ultradian Rhythms In Life Processes: A Fundamental Inquiry Into Chronobiology and Psychobiology*, New York: Springer-Verlag.
McGilchrist, I, *The Master and his Emissary*, 2009, Yale University Press.
Mitchell, S. A., 2000, *Relationality: From Attachment to Intersubjectivity*, The Analytic Press.
Orsucci, F., 2009, *Mind Force: On Human Attractions*, World Scientific..
Panksepp, J., 2005, *Affective Neuroscience: The Foundations Of Human And Animal Emotions*, Oxford University Press.
Panksepp, J., 2008, *The Blackwell Companion To Consciousness: Affective Consciousness*, Blackwell Publishing.
Pinker, S., 2002, *Blank Slate: The modern denial of human nature*, Penguin Books.
Rossi E. L., *The Psychobiology of Mind-Body Healing*, 1993, Norton.
Rossi, E. L., 2000, *Dreams, Consciousness, Spirit: The Quantum Experience Of Self-Reflection and Co-Creation*, Zeig, Tucker & Theisen Inc.
Rossi, E. L., 2002, *The Psychobiology of Gene Expression: Neuroscience And Neurogenesis In Hypnosis And The Healing Arts*, W.W. Norton and Company Inc.
Rowan, D., 2009a, *Is there a basis in neuroscience in NLP: reflections on my practice from my participation in the AES programme*, unpublished.
Rowan, D., 2009b, *A place to belong: investigating the relationship between landscape and identity*, unpublished.
Rowan, D., 2009c, *Forming an attachment to attachment theory: a journal of an emergent understanding*, unpublished.

Rowan, D., *What roles may discourse, narrative and literalism play in the making and resolution of conflict*, unpublished.

Sasportas, H., 1985, *The Twelve Houses*, Aquarian press.

Schore, A.N., 1994, *Affect Regulation and the Origin of the Self; The Neurobiology of Emotional Development*, Lawrence Erlbaum Associates, Publishers.

Schore, A. N., 2003, *Affect Dysregulation And Disorders Of The Self*, W.W. Norton and Company Inc.

Schore, A. N., 2003, *Affect Regulation And The Repair Of The Self*, W.W. Norton and Company Inc.

Sheldrake, R., 2003, *The Sense of Being Stared At: And Other Aspects Of The Extended Mind*, Hutchinson.

Sibley, D., 1995, *Geographies of Exclusion*, Routeledge.

Spence, S. A., 2009, *The Actor's Brain*, Oxford University Press.

Tester, J., 1987, *A History of Western Astrology*, The Boydell Press.

Trevarthen, C., Reddy, V., 2008, *The Blackwell Companion To Consciousness: Consciousness in Infants*, Blackwell Publishing.

Trevarthen, C. , 2003, *Revolutionary Connections: Psychotherapy and Neuroscience: Neuroscience and intrinsic psychodynamics: current knowledge and potential for therapy*, Karnac

Trimble, M. R., 2007, *The Soul In The Brain*, The Johns Hopkins University Press.

Waterfield, R., 2002, *Hidden Depths: The Story of Hypnosis*, Macmillan.

Watt, F., 2003, *Revolutionary Connections: Psychotherapy in an age of neuroscience: bridges to affective neuroscience*, H. Karnac Books Ltd.

Vaerela, F. J., Thompson, E., Rosch, E., 1993, *The Embodied Mind: Cognitive Science and Human Experience*, The MIT Press.

Post Script

It is now five years since I completed the Master of Science in Psycho-Social Studies and I am rather proud to say I was awarded a distinction for the degree.

The experience of the course has literally been life changing; the focus of my research since 2008 has been Affective Neuroscience and Interpersonal Neurobiology. During my time on the course I noticed that my private consultancy practice had changed and my Client work had become more confident, congruent and competent.

The insights I gained from exploring these perspectives has filtered through into all my other work as well; from teaching astrology online to the honing of my craft in guiding people around the Neolithic landscapes of Avebury and Stonehenge, my understanding of Affect and Mirror Neurons, Bion's third way and utilising the environment and landscape as a secure base, the ripples have been far reaching and their transformative effects profound.

My understanding of my own position as an adult with Aspergers Syndrome, Dyslexia, Dyspraxia and Echo-praxia, is clearer and I have been told I have profoundly touched parents of other people who live in the spectrum.

The concepts and depth of understanding gleaned from taking this path have brought an incredible light of illumination into my life. I am very grateful to the Psycho-Social Studies unit at UWE for giving me the opportunity to study with them. It was an extraordinary privilege and I hope that you too find such a light of illumination here.

David Charles Rowan, March 2015.

Printed in Poland
by Amazon Fulfillment
Poland Sp. z o.o., Wrocław

60790128R00116